PRESIDENTS AT WAR

HOW
GEORGE W. BUSH
FOUGHT THE
WARS IN IRAQ
AND
AFGHANISTAN

PRESIDENTS
AT WAR

HOW
GEORGE W.
BUSH
FOUGHT THE
WARS IN IRAQ
AND
AFGHANISTAN

Don Rauf

Enslow Publishing
101 W. 23rd Street
Suite 240
New York, NY 10011
USA

enslow.com

Published in 2018 by Enslow Publishing, LLC.
101 W. 23rd Street, Suite 240, New York, NY 10011

Library of Congress Cataloging-in-Publication Data

Names: Rauf, Don, author.
  Title: How George W. Bush fought the wars in Iraq and Afghanistan /
    Don Rauf.
  Description: New York : Enslow Publishing, 2018. | Series: Presidents at war |
    Includes bibliographical references and index. | Audience: Grades 7-12.
  Identifiers: LCCN 2017003128 | ISBN 9780766085336 (library-bound)
  Subjects: LCSH: Bush, George W. (George Walker), 1946– —Military leadership—
    Juvenile literature. | War on Terrorism, 2001–2009—Juvenile literature. | Afghan
    War, 2001—Juvenile literature. | Iraq War, 2003–2011—Juvenile literature. |
    United States—Foreign relations—2001–2009—Juvenile literature. | United
    States—Politics and government—2001–2009—Juvenile literature.
  Classification: LCC E903.3.R38 2017 | DDC 973.931092 [B]—dc23
  LC record available at https://lccn.loc.gov/2017003128

Printed in the United States of America

To Our Readers: We have done our best to make sure all website addresses in this
book were active and appropriate when we went to press. However, the author and the
publisher have no control over and assume no liability for the material available on
those websites or on any websites they may link to. Any comments or suggestions can
be sent by e-mail to customerservice@enslow.com.

Photo Credits: Cover, pp. 1, 3, 7, 10, 25, 37, 51, 61, 71, 83, 95 Eric Draper,
photographer, courtesy of the George Bush Presidential Library; cover, pp. 3, 80 Ramzi
Haidar/AFP/Getty Images; p. 6 Spencer Platt/Getty Images; p. 11 © AP Images; p. 19
Steve Elfers/The LIFE Picture Collection/Getty Images; p. 23 Mark Wilson/Hulton
Archive/Getty Images; p. 26 CNN/Getty Images; p. 28 Paul J. Richards/AFP/Getty
Images; p. 41 Universal Images Group/Getty Images; p. 43 Benjamin Lowy/Getty
Images; p. 45 Sean Gallup/Getty Images; pp. 48, 67 Joe Raedle/Getty Images; p. 53
STRDEL/AFP/Getty Images; p. 55 Paula Bronstein/Getty Images; p. 57 John Moore/
Getty Images; pp. 58, 79 U.S. Navy/Getty Images; p. 62 Chip HIRES/Gamma-
Rapho/Getty Images; p. 72 Stephen Chernin/Getty Images; p. 77 Getty Images; p. 81
ullstein bild/Getty Images; p. 84 Stephen Jaffe/AFP/Getty Images; p. 89 AFP/Getty
Images; p. 92 Antonio Scorza/AFP/Getty Images; p. 93 Ali Al-Saadi/AFP/Getty
Images; p. 96 Saul Loeb/AFP/Getty Images; p. 98 Ulrich Baumgarten/Getty Images.

CONTENTS

After two hijacked airplanes slammed into the twin towers in New York on September 11, 2001, President George W. Bush initiated the war on terror.

INTRODUCTION

When George W. Bush was president of the United States, between 2001 and 2009, the United States entered a war unlike any it had ever encountered before. This was a war on terror, and while it was to be fought against specific regimes in Afghanistan and Iraq, it was also going to be waged everywhere in the world, as the United States and other countries attempted to stop acts of terrorism wherever they might occur.

The wars of George W. Bush, the forty-third president of the United States, were brought on by a cataclysmic event—the attacks by terrorists on American soil on September 11, 2001. Terrorist acts by Islamic extremists had been increasing around the world throughout the Bill Clinton administration, prior to George W. Bush becoming president. From the moment of 9/11, Bush's top priority was to protect Americans from "evildoers." Bush said later that the moment he realized the country was under attack, US foreign policy quickly changed direction: from one of little intervention to one in which America would take aggressive action to destroy terrorists and prevent further hostile actions toward the country.

In the days following the attacks, President Bush showed the calm, resolve, and strength that the country desperately needed to carry on. He did a masterful job speaking to all citizens in a moment of crisis, and his popularity rose to an all-time high. His call to Americans was to remain calm and carry on, to show the terrorists that Americans would not let these actions deter them from their normal lives. Some criticized him for urging people to go shopping and take vacations during this time of crisis, but others saw his words as encouragement to not to be intimidated by terrorists and to refuse to live lives led by fear.

Even in his first inaugural address in January 2001, Bush made clear his objectives for the nation: "If our country does not lead the cause of freedom, it will not be led. If we do not turn the hearts of children toward knowledge and character, we will lose their gifts and undermine their idealism. If we permit our economy to drift and decline, the vulnerable will suffer most."[1]

To fight back against Osama bin Laden, the mastermind of the attacks, the United States entered the longest war in American history. On December 28, 2014, President Barack Obama called an official end to the combat mission,[2] although a number of troops continue to "keep the peace" in the region. The harsh regime of the Taliban, which protected bin Laden, was eliminated as the ruling power, and a new democratic government was established. The people in the region now had more opportunities for education, work, health care, and more. But even at the end of 2016, Taliban forces were been fighting back and regaining territory. In November of that year, two American servicemen were killed and four were wounded on a mission with the Afghan military to clear a Taliban position and disrupt the group's operations in the Kunduz district.[3]

In a more controversial move, President Bush took the war on terror into Iraq. Bush launched a preemptive strike against Saddam Hussein, convinced that he had weapons of mass destruction, although these weapons never materialized. Saddam was a merciless dictator who severely limited personal freedoms. When Bush toppled Saddam Hussein's regime, he established a democratic government in Iraq, but a strong insurgent movement rose in the region and American troops suffered more than four thousand deaths over the course of eight years.

Bush's presidency was controversial right from the beginning. During the 2000 election, his opponent, Al Gore, won the popular vote. The difference in the popular vote in Florida was razor thin. The US Supreme Court, however, stopped a recount of votes in Florida, despite Bush having just a 537-vote lead in the state. This meant Bush won the election. Former Bush speechwriter David Frum said that no matter what Bush went through, he had perseverance and tenacity that propelled him forward. "There is a kind of personal stubbornness that makes him take hold of something, and not let it go," he said. Bush told journalist Bob Woodward, "I'm a gut player. I play by instincts. I don't play by the book."[4] Wayne Slater, the bureau chief for the *Dallas Morning News* in Austin, said that Bush had absolute confidence in his ability to get something done, and that's how he proceeded throughout his presidency and through two wars, which have brought more freedoms to Iraq and Afghanistan but have not eliminated the instability in these regions.

THE AGE OF TERRORISM BEGINS

George W. Bush's job approval rating following September 11 was 90 percent, higher than the approval rating received by Franklin Roosevelt after Pearl Harbor.

For President George Bush, the wars in Iraq and Afghanistan had their beginning moments in a calm and innocent setting. On the morning of September 11, 2001, Bush was scheduled to visit the students in Sandra Kay Daniel's second-grade class at the Emma E. Booker Elementary School in Sarasota, Florida. It was a minor event to promote his educational initiative "No Child Left Behind." Bush was in an upbeat mood, and he told his chief of staff, Andrew Card, "It should be an easy day." The students, many from struggling families, were also in a good mood, excited to meet the president. To help develop their reading skills, Ms. Daniel had her children reading a short, simple book called *The Pet Goat*.

White House chief of staff Andrew Card whispered the news about the World Trade Center attacks to George W. Bush as he read before a grade school class in Florida.

Shortly before 9 a.m., presidential staff learned that a plane had crashed into one of the two towers at the World Trade Center.[1] Initially, people thought that it might be a small aircraft, perhaps caused by pilot error. Nobody knew at that moment that a major airliner had crashed into the North Tower. In 2001, there were no iPhones or Black-berries, so communication was a bit more difficult. Bush's press secretary Ari Fleischer said in an interview in *Politico Magazine*, "I had this high-tech pager on my belt—it was two-way, in that you could send back one of like 14 prepro-grammed responses. For the day, it was pretty fancy-fancy stuff."[2]

The president and his staff decided to stay informed and move ahead with their presentation until they could learn more. The president sat ready to read *The Pet Goat*, and the teacher asked her students to take out their books. Then at 9:03 a.m., United Airlines Flight 175, with 65 aboard, struck the South Tower of the World Trade Center.

When Andrew Card received the message, he knew this was more than an accident. He walked up to the president, who was in front of the classroom before the students, all focused on their books. Card whispered in his ear, "A second plane hit the second tower. America is under attack."[3] Bush kept his calm to not alarm anyone. He told the students he had to leave, and the staff rushed him off to Air Force One, the presidential jet.

As the morning progressed, the country realized that the attack was bigger than the horrific jet crashes into the World Trade Center towers. American Airlines Flight 77 crashed into the Pentagon at 9:37 a.m.; and then, at just after 10 a.m., United Airlines Flight 93 dove full speed into an empty field in Shanksville, Pennsylvania, twenty minutes from Washington, DC. Some passengers on that flight decided to fight back against the hijackers. Their actions may have saved many lives on the ground. Fearing that the passengers would break through the cockpit door, the hijacker piloting Flight 93 aimed the plane toward the ground as voices chanted, "Allah is great!" Although the intended target was never fully determined, many suspected that it was either the White House or the Capitol Building.

When the attacks were over, more than three thousand people had been killed, including more than four hundred police officers and firefighters. During the chaotic day, Vice President Dick Cheney gave orders to shoot down any commercial jet believed to have been hijacked.

It was clear that America was under siege. As the president and staff assessed what was happening, Bush flew to different military bases to assure his safety. The Federal Aviation Administration told all planes in the sky over the continental United States to land. They were all guided to nearby airports. (For three days after the attack, the skies over America were empty.)

Calming a Shocked Nation

Bush knew he would now have to take on one of the most serious roles of the president—that of chief of the armed forces. That night President Bush addressed a nation that was living in sudden fear, shock, and uncertainty. He had to appear before the nation and offer strength, courage, and calm. He told America:

Today, our fellow citizens, our way of life, our very freedom came under attack in a series of deliberate and deadly terrorist acts. The victims were in airplanes or in their offices—secretaries, businessmen and women, military and federal workers. Moms and dads. Friends and neighbors. Thousands of lives were suddenly ended by evil, despicable acts of terror.

Our country is strong. A great people has been moved to defend a great nation. Terrorist attacks can shake the foundations of our biggest buildings, but they cannot touch the foundation of America. These acts shatter steel, but they cannot dent the steel of American resolve.

This is a day when all Americans from every walk of life unite in our resolve for justice and peace. America has stood down enemies before, and we will do so this time. None of us will ever forget this day, yet we go forward to defend freedom and all that is good and just in our world.[4]

After 9/11, the United States and the world entered a new type of war—the war against terrorism.

The Link to al-Qaeda and Osama bin Laden

From intelligence reports, Bush and his national defense team were almost certain that these assaults on America were the work of al-Qaeda. Terrorist acts by al-Qaeda had been building for years since the Bill Clinton administration in 1990s. Osama bin Laden was the leader of this Islamic extremist group, and he took credit for countless horrific acts. Bin Laden had formed the terrorist network in the mid-1980s. The 9/11 Museum explains that the goal of al-Qaeda was to overthrow governments in the Middle East and elsewhere in the Muslim world.[5] His group wanted to carry out a jihad or, in their view, a violent struggle needed to eradicate obstacles to restoring God's rule on Earth. But, by far, the majority of Muslims disavow violence and terror.

Al-Qaeda targeted countries that did not strictly enforce a political and social order that they believed was essential to Islam. Attacks against the United States were intended to reduce American support for many of these governments; US support was viewed by al-Qaeda as a major obstacle to creating a global order under Islamic authority. The movement took root in Afghanistan in the 1980s. At that time, Osama bin Laden, who was from a wealthy family in Saudi Arabia, joined forces in Afghanistan to fight the invading Soviet Union. He used some of his family fortune to assist the Afghan struggle.[6] The Soviet Union signed a peace accord and began to pull out in 1988, but that did not bring peace to the nation. The country then entered a long civil war. The fundamentalist Islamic militia called the Taliban (which literally means "the Seekers") eventually took control by 1996, and by 1997, Pakistan and Saudi Arabia recognized the Taliban as the legitimate rulers of Afghanistan.[7]

This very hard-line regime imposed rigid enforcement of Islamic law. Violence between warring factions ended, but so did many personal freedoms. Television, the internet, music, photography, playing cards, computer disks, movies, satellite TV, musical instruments, and chess-boards were all outlawed.[8] Punishments for crimes were severe, ranging from amputations to deadly stonings. The Taliban committed many human rights abuses against its own people—women, girls, and Hazaras (a Persian-speaking people who mainly live in central Afghanistan) were often targeted. Working women were threatened and forced to quit their jobs. They had to maintain strict dress codes or be punished. The citizens of Afghanistan were living under devastating poverty. An article on the History Channel website estimated that up to four million people were suffering from starvation under Taliban rule.[9]

Bin Laden worked with the Taliban to construct a complex of training camps for the purpose of creating terrorists who could successfully carry out suicide bombings and armed combat. His movement was called al-Qaeda, or "the Base." He then initiated or inspired attacks against the United States and Western allies in the 1990s when Bill Clinton was president. On February 23, 1993, a truck bomb was detonated in an underground garage in the World Trade Center, killing six. In the summer of that year, FBI agents thwarted a plan to bomb tunnels and bridges, the Statue of Liberty, the United Nations, and other sites in New York. Extremists worked to mount an assassination attempt on Bill Clinton in 1994. In 1995, police in the Philippines stopped a plan to blow up several US airplanes.[10] With these terrorist attacks growing, President Clinton put forth the first Presidential Decision Directive labeling terrorism "a national security issue" in June of 1995.

More terrorist acts followed. In 1996, a truck bomb went off at the Khobar Towers complex in Saudi Arabia, killing nineteen American servicemen and wounding four hundred. In 1998, suicide bombers murdered 240 people in Tanzania and Kenya, including twelve Americans. Off the coast of Yemen in 2000, a small boat exploded near the US warship *Cole*, killing seventeen US sailors and wounding scores more. Clinton authorized the CIA to track down and kill Osama bin Laden, but despite his efforts the terrorist leader remained elusive. In 1998, Clinton's secretary of defense, William Cohen, asked that a congressional commission be put together to conduct a comprehensive review of US national security requirements in the twenty-first century. Their report concluded that "America will be attacked by terrorists using weapons of mass destruction, and Americans will die, possibly in large numbers, on American soil."[11] That same year, Clinton authorized covert action against bin Laden and al-Qaeda.

With all these terrorist acts occurring during the presidency of Bill Clinton, George W. Bush was aware that more assaults might be coming when he became president. In fact, on September 10, the day before the 9/11 attacks, the Bush administration's top national security officials met to discuss how to get rid of Osama bin Laden. According to a report in the *Guardian*, they decided that the Taliban in Afghanistan would be presented with a final ultimatum: They had to turn in bin Laden and if they refused, the United States would send support to anti-Taliban groups. Then if those efforts were unsuccessful, "the deputies agreed that the United States would seek to overthrow the Taliban regime through more direct action."[12]

George H. W. Bush's War on Iraq

Even before Bill Clinton and George W. Bush began working to stop bin Laden, George Herbert Walker Bush—George W. Bush's father and the president before Bill Clinton took office—had foreseen danger arising from the dictatorship of Saddam Hussein in Iraq, a volatile country in the Middle East. George H. W. Bush battled Saddam in 1990. When nearby oil-rich Kuwait would not forgive the debts taken on by Iraq from a previous war with Iran, Saddam proceeded to invade Kuwait. At this point, Saddam had a fairly large military force of one million men, although it is estimated that only one-third were professionally trained and ready to fight. Iraq took Kuwait City and headed toward the border of Saudi Arabia. During their few months controlling Kuwait, the Iraqis committed crimes against humanity that went against the Laws of Armed Conflict as outlined in the Geneva and Hague Conventions. They tortured civilians to the point of disfigurement or death. Because Kuwait was an ally of the United States as well as the second-largest source of petroleum in the Middle East, George H. W. Bush started the Persian Gulf War, code-named Operation Desert Shield. At first, US forces bombed Iraq and its troops.

On February 24, 1991, after six weeks of heavy bombing, the US forces set forth on a ground operation called Operation Desert Storm. Forces from thirty-two nations took part, including Britain, Egypt, France, Saudi Arabia, and Kuwait. The coalition forces numbered about 750,000. United States general Norman Schwarzkopf led the troops into battle, although he said later that war was the last thing he wanted. He hoped Saddam would surrender upon seeing the sheer might he was up against.[13, 14]

President George H. W. Bush led the US to war against Iraq in early 1991 after Saddam Hussein invaded Kuwait.

In an interview, Schwarzkopf said, "I hate war. Absolutely, I hate war. Good generalship is a realization that … you've got to try and figure out how to accomplish your mission with a minimum loss of human life. When the war started, we were hoping that they'd come to their senses and stop right then."[15]

Saddam knew he was outnumbered but he tried a long-shot strategy. He declared a jihad and launched missiles into Israel and Saudi Arabia. He thought if these countries entered the battle, Iraq would find other allies to join his side.

But Saddam's strategy attracted no support. Plus, US-military might and state-of-the-art weapons totally dominated with stealth bombers, cruise missiles, so-called smart bombs with laser-guidance systems, and infrared night-bombing equipment. Iraqi forces attempted to fight back, but they quickly were forced out of Kuwait. Four days after the ground battle began, the war was over. The land war lasted all of one hundred hours. A total of three hundred coalition troops lost their lives compared to about eight thousand to ten thousand Iraqi soldiers.

Bush Sr. decided to accept a truce without removing Saddam from power. He thought forcing Saddam from power would go against the UN Security Council. Also, different factions and factors in the region made it a difficult decision to know what would lead to the greatest peace and stability. George H. W. Bush did sign a secret action giving the CIA authority to topple Saddam, and the United States encouraged uprisings against Saddam.[16]

After the war ended, gas prices doubled, and the United States went into a recession as the economy plunged. So despite George H. W. Bush's success and popularity, Americans voted for a change with a hope for more jobs and a better economy.[17] When Bill Clinton was elected in 1992, Saddam was still a threat and was brutally attacking those who threatened his regime—particularly the Kurdish people to the north and the Shiites to the south.

The Democrat Bill Clinton along with support from Congress signed the Iraq Liberation Act of 1998. Clinton wrote: "This Act makes clear that it is the sense of the Congress that the United States should support those elements of the Iraqi opposition that advocate a very different future for Iraq than the bitter reality of internal repression and external aggression that the current regime in Baghdad now offers."[18] Ousting Saddam was a goal, but Clinton did not actively pursue it. He did, however, warn that Saddam must be carefully monitored so as not to "build arsenals of nuclear, chemical and biological weapons and the missiles to deliver them."

Bush, the Son, Takes the Reins

Because of the divisiveness of the 2000 election, Republican George W. Bush, son of the forty-first president, started his new job as the leader of America determined to work together with Democrats. He told all American citizens: "I'm here to tell the country that things will get done, that we're going to rise above expectations, that both Republicans and Democrats will come together to do what's right for America."[20] Congress was fairly evenly divided, so it was difficult to get much done. But one mission unified all: protecting the United States from any terrorist attacks. Coming into the job in the new millennium, Bush knew stopping terrorism would be a high priority.

In spring of 2001, Bush's national security advisor, Condoleezza Rice, had received some warning that al-Qaeda cells might be forming on American soil, but these forces could not be tracked down. There was a growing sense that some sort of major attack might be

The Highly Contested Election of 2000

When George W. Bush won the election against Al Gore in 2000, the outcome was highly disputed because the results were very close in Florida. In the end, the presidency came down to 537 votes, which made the difference. The battle over the counting eventually was ended by the Supreme Court. The divided court ruled that Florida's manual recount of vote ballots was unconstitutional. The recount was declared unconstitutional because it granted more protection to some ballots than to others. So in the end Bush won the most electoral votes from the states (271 to 266), but Gore won the popular vote (50,999,897 to 50,456,002). With the country divided and the final outcome in question for many, Bush had to bring the nation together with his inauguration speech. Bush thanked Gore "for a contest conducted with spirit and ended with grace."

He reached out to all Americans saying "that everyone belongs, that everyone deserves a chance, that no insignificant person was ever born." He went on to say, "Our unity, our Union, is a serious work of leaders and citizens and every generation. And this is my solemn pledge: I will work to build a single nation of justice and opportunity."[19] Although he took this step toward unity and won many supporters, he still faced many who felt the election was unfairly decided.

Demonstrators protested outside of the Supreme Court when justices heard arguments about the vote recount in Florida in 2000.

coming, but the government was unable to uncover the plot. CIA director George Tenet said, "The system was blinking red." In August 2001, he was presented with a briefing titled "Islamic Extremist Learns to Fly." Tenet later testified: "We all understood bin Laden's intent to strike the homeland but were unable to translate this knowledge into an effective defense of the country."[21] On August 16, 2001, the FBI arrested French citizen Zacharias Moussaoui and charged him with an immigration violation. The FBI was also suspicious of his intentions when they discovered that he had taken flight training courses in Eagan, Minnesota.

He later pleaded guilty in US federal court to conspiring to kill citizens of the United States as part of the 9/11 attacks.

But at this time, US security advisors could not quite put the pieces together that terrorists could already be on home soil planning attacks. Still, for George W. Bush, Osama bin Laden was a known threat, and Bush was reviewing a plan with the CIA to use armed remote-controlled planes to hunt him down and kill him. After 9/11, the United States under George Bush would launch a war against terrorism, bin Laden, and any countries George W. Bush's administration perceived as a threat.

CHAPTER TWO

SETTING THE STAGE FOR WAR

Six days after 9/11, Bush visited a Washington mosque and spoke against the harassment of Arabs and Muslims living in the United States and the need to respect Islam.

Within days of the attacks of September 11, 2001, it was clear who the nineteen hijackers were. They made almost no effort to hide their identities, buying plane tickets under their true names. Fifteen of the hijackers were from Saudi Arabia, two were from the United Arab Emirates, one was from Egypt, and one was from Lebanon.[1] Evidence was soon found that those who carried out the terrorist attacks were connected with al-Qaeda, so Bush's most pressing mission became the destruction of al-Qaeda and the capture or killing of Osama bin Laden, who was the leader of the terrorist group.

When Osama bin Laden admitted to planning the 9/11 attacks, he became the number one target in the US war on terror.

But ahead of all other matters, Bush had to set about reassuring a nation struck by fear and uncertainty. On September 14, he led a national prayer service at the National Cathedral in Washington, DC, attended by all the former living presidents. As Americans learned that the terrorist acts were the work of Islamic extremists, Bush was concerned that there would be unfounded hostility toward Muslim Americans. To subdue any backlash, President Bush visited the Washington Islamic Center and urged all Americans to work together and not to show any hatred or discrimination to Muslims or Arabs. "These acts of violence against innocents violate the fundamental tenets of the Islamic faith," Bush said. "And it's important for my fellow Americans to understand that … the face of terror is not the true faith of Islam. That's not what Islam is all about. Islam is peace."[2] Muslim American and Arab American political organizations all immediately denounced the September 11 attacks.

Three days after the attack, Bush arrived at the site of devastation brought on by the two airliners that toppled the twin towers, an area that quickly became known as Ground Zero. Stepping among the construction crew and rescue workers, Bush grabbed a bullhorn and told the enthusiastic crowd, "I can hear you. The rest of the world hears you. And the people who knocked down these buildings will hear all of us soon. The nation sends its love and compassion to everybody who's here. Thank you for your hard work. Thank you for making the nation proud, and may God bless America."[3]

The country rallied behind Bush. His standings in Gallup polls before 9/11 were just about 50 percent, from a nation that was widely divided after the hotly contested election. But shortly after the attacks his popularity numbers soared to 90 percent.[4] Both political parties and the press praised his strength and the actions he was taking to unite the country and to fight terrorism.

Targeting Afghanistan and the Taliban

Americans wanted to fight back against those responsible— but who would be the targets? It was more and more clear that al-Qaeda was responsible. Afghanistan, under the strict Taliban regime, allowed al-Qaeda and bin Laden to train terrorists in the country, so Bush and his advisors started to develop plans to attack the country and destroy al-Qaeda

George W. Bush buoyed the nation when he spoke to rescue volunteers and firemen through a bullhorn at Ground Zero on September 14, 2001.

operations there. The United States would not go it alone either. One day after the attacks, the member nations of the North Atlantic Treaty Organization (NATO) issued a statement agreeing to come together to help fight those who attacked the United States. NATO cited Article 5 of the treaty, saying that an armed attack against one or more of the allies in Europe or North America should be considered an attack against them all.[5] The sense of unity with Europe and other free nations was expressed in the headline on September 12 in the French paper *Le Monde*: "We Are All Americans."

The weekend after the attacks, Bush and his cabinet had a lot of strategizing to do and decisions to make. They gathered together at Camp David, the 143-acre (58-hectare) country retreat of the president, in the Catoctin Mountains of Maryland—about 70 miles (112 kilometers) from the White House. Laura Bush, the president's wife, recalled the weekend as one of high emotion and anxiety. They weighed three different options. The United States could use cruise missiles (a type of guided missile that can be fired over long distances with great accuracy) to hit al-Qaeda camps, but President Clinton had followed a similar course and it did not eliminate bin Laden. They could increase the assault to include both cruise missiles and bombers and destroy a wider range of targets. But George Bush wrote in his book *Decision Points* that he felt these options would be ineffective: "This time we would put boots on the ground, and keep them there until the Taliban and al-Qaeda were driven out and a free society could emerge."

In Bush's inner circle, there was also debate whether it was the right time to strike at Iraq, which was still perceived as a threat by some. Since the 2000 election, Saddam's removal had been part of the Republican platform. The deputy secretary of defense, Paul Wolfowitz, was pushing for immediate action against Iraq, according to James Mann's biography on George W. Bush. Secretary of State Colin Powell opposed this move because he thought countries needed to focus their efforts on uniting against the Taliban in Afghanistan. National Security Advisor Condoleezza Rice and Vice President Cheney also backed the approach to shelve the Iraq problem for the time being and to concentrate on al-Qaeda. Bush wrote later in his biography, "Unless I received definitive evidence tying Saddam Hussein to the 9/11 plot, I would work to resolve the Iraq problem diplomatically. I hoped unified pressure by the world might compel Saddam to meet international obligations. The best way to show him we were serious was to succeed in Afghanistan."[6]

The President Addresses a Shaken Nation

Bush scheduled a speech for September 20 in front of a joint session of Congress, when both the House of Representatives and the Senate gather together. To show that the world was uniting in its efforts to fight back against al-Qaeda, Bush invited British prime minister Tony Blair to join him for this important speech. Bush was bolstered by Blair's vow that Great Britain would be at America's side. More than eighty-two million people around the world were watching.

Bush warned that the battle would be lengthy: "Our response involves far more than instant retaliation and

New Airline Security Rules

At the same time that Bush was deciding on what courses of action to take, America was slowly coming back to life. For two days, the skies over America remained eerily silent. Flights slowly began on Thursday, September 13.[7] Many restrictions and security measures were quickly put in place. Secretary of Transportation Norm Mineta announced more law enforcement at airports. Sharp tools, even small jackknives, would no longer be allowed on aircraft. Based on reports from those aboard the hijacked planes who were able to make phone calls, it was thought that the hijackers might have used knives or box cutters to overtake the crew, the reason for such concern over small knives and sharp items. Barbara Olson, a conservative television reporter, was aboard American Flight 77 on September 11, heading to California to tape an episode of Bill Maher's television show, *Politically Incorrect*. She reported that hijackers were carrying knives and box cutters, but she did not describe how they got into the cockpit. An attendant aboard Flight 11 said that hijackers disabled her with a toxic spray.

Just over two months after the attacks, Congress federalized airport security by passing the Aviation and Transportation Security Act on November 19. The act formed the new Transportation Security

Continued on the next page

Continued from the previous page

Administration (TSA). Each airport had handled its own security before 9/11, using their own private companies to enforce security, but now the new TSA created national guidelines for passenger and luggage screening. Passengers with tickets would be the only ones allowed through security.

Updated screening equipment was installed to scan for weapons and any other possible destructive items. As new threats were discovered after 9/11, new procedures were introduced, including limiting any liquids to 3.4-ounce containers. On December 22, 2001, Richard Reid tried to ignite explosives hidden in his shoes on a flight from Paris to Miami. As a result, TSA began requesting that people remove their shoes and send them through screening devices. After Umar Farouk Abdulmutallab tried to blow up Northwest Flight 253 with a bomb hidden in his underwear, TSA called for full-body scanners, and by December 2010 newly advanced imaging technology was put in place.[8]

isolated strikes. Americans should not expect one battle, but a lengthy campaign, unlike any other we have ever seen. It may include dramatic strikes, visible on TV, and covert operations, secret even in success … Every nation, in every region now has a decision to make. Either you are with us, or you are with the terrorists."

He also gave the Taliban an ultimatum: "They will hand over the terrorists, or they will share in their fate." His speech included this inspirational sentence: "We will not tire, we will not falter, and we will not fail." And he assured all citizens: "I will not forget this wound to our country or those who inflicted it. I will not yield; I will not rest; I will not relent in waging this struggle for freedom and security for the American people."[9]

On September 22, 2001, the ruling Taliban ignored an edict by Islamic clerics requesting that Osama bin Laden leave the country, defying America's demands that they hand him over or face military strikes. President Bush had also said that the Taliban must give up senior al-Qaeda members and close all terrorist training camps inside Afghanistan. The Taliban refused on all counts.

Worries on the Home Front and the Patriot Act

Compounding matters on the home front was an anthrax scare. Anthrax is a serious infectious disease. Seven days after the terrorist attacks of September 11, 2001, anonymous letters laced with deadly anthrax spores began arriving at media companies and congressional offices. Over the next two months, five people died from inhaling anthrax and seventeen more were infected from exposure. In 2010, the FBI, the Department of Justice, and the US Postal Inspection Service concluded that government scientist Dr. Bruce Ivins was responsible. He was a senior biodefense researcher at the United States Army Medical Research

Securing the Homeland

Bush's speech before Congress after 9/11 also outlined his plan to create the US Department of Homeland Security. Two days after Bush delivered this speech before Congress, he appointed Pennsylvania governor Tom Ridge as the first director of the Office of Homeland Security. Bush chose Ridge because he was a capable governor of Pennsylvania, a military veteran, and a trusted friend. Ridge worked with more than 180,000 employees from a combined twenty-two components to come together as one agency to strengthen borders, provide for intelligence analysis and infrastructure protection, improve the use of science and technology to counter weapons of mass destruction, and create a comprehensive response and recovery division.

Ridge served as the nation's first secretary of Homeland Security until February 1, 2005. Under his direction, the Office of Homeland Security developed a color-coded terrorism threat advisory scale called the Homeland Security Advisory System. For example, green was low, yellow was elevated, and red was severe. The level was raised to red only once for about a month's time, in August to September 2006, when British intelligence received informaton about a plot to blow up aircraft. The color-code warning system was later phased out under President Barack Obama. In his book *The Test of Our Times: America Under Siege ... and How We Can Be Safe Again,* Ridge said he was pressured to raise the terror alert level on the eve of the 2004 presidential election, although he said he refused to do so.[10]

Institute of Infectious Diseases, Fort Detrick, Maryland. He had committed suicide in 2008. [11]

On October 26, 2001, Congress passed the USA Patriot Act, which gave more authority to the Justice Department and to the FBI so there would be an improved connection between intelligence collection and law enforcement. The law gave the government more powers to spy on citizens by expanding the authority to monitor phone and email communications, collect bank and credit reporting records, examine leases and library records, and track the activity of citizens on the internet. Prior to the act, the FBI would need permission from a judge to carry out such acts.

People have been divided over the act because supporters believe it to be crucial for uncovering terrorist plots, but critics think the act gives the government too much power, puts civil liberties at risk, and threatens the very democracy it seeks to protect. Some say that the Patriot Act violates the First Amendment, which upholds our rights to freedom of expression, speech, and information. Critics say that people lose the right to say what and how they truly feel because they can be prosecuted for it. Some say it also goes against the Fourth Amendment of the Constitution of the United States, which guarantees, "The right of the people to be secure in their persons, houses, papers, and effects, against unreasonable searches and seizures, shall not be violated, and no Warrants shall issue, but upon probable cause, supported by Oath or affirmation, and particularly describing the place to be searched, and the persons or things to be seized." [12]

The actions, though, were prompted by the fact that al-Qaeda was able to secretly get agents to operate for it in the United States, and that these agents were able to communicate with al-Qaeda in Afghanistan. FBI director Robert S. Mueller wrote in 2004, "The terrorist threat presents complex challenges. Terrorists move easily across international borders, use sophisticated technology to recruit, network, and communicate, and finance their operations with elaborate funding schemes. Above all, they are patient. They are methodical. They are determined to succeed."

He indicated that intelligence-gathering capabilities allowed under the Patriot Act have enabled the FBI to disrupt terrorist plans and to fight the war on terror. On its website, the Justice Department wrote that its "first priority is to prevent future terrorist attacks. Since its passage following the September 11, 2001 attacks, the Patriot Act has played a key part—and often the leading role— in a number of successful operations to protect innocent Americans from the deadly plans of terrorists dedicated to destroying America and our way of life."[13]

CHAPTER THREE

THE BATTLE AGAINST THE TALIBAN

Bush was proud to have Hamid Karzai become the first democratically elected leader in the five-thousand-year history of Afghanistan.

Bush needed a military leader to carry out plans to attack Afghanistan, assuming that the Taliban would not hand over bin Laden. Bush chose four-star general Tommy Franks to lead the mission. Franks had grown up in Midland, Texas, and attended the same high school as Bush's wife, Laura. He was a highly regarded commander who had served in Vietnam and led troops in the first Gulf War. He was in the top position in the US military commanding an area that stretched from the Horn of Africa to central Asia, including Afghanistan.[1]

In meetings with General Franks, Bush knew that waging war in Afghanistan would be difficult. Bush wrote in *Decisions Points* that Afghanistan was "remote, rugged, and primitive." He described the landscape as desolate and foreboding. "Its northern half is home to ethnic Tajiks, Uzbeks, Hazaras, Turkmen, and others. The southern half is dominated by Pashtuns. Tribal, ethnic, and religious rivalries date back centuries. Yet for all their differences, the people of Afghanistan have a way of banding together against foreigners."[2] Some Afghan civilians warned that America's threats might act to unite the public behind the Taliban, even though they were living under the oppression of harsh Islamic laws.

They developed a four-stage war plan that would be dubbed Operation Enduring Freedom. First, Special Forces and CIA teams would go in and secure some space and establish a base for additional troops. Then the Taliban and al-Qaeda would be subject to heavy bombing. Humanitarian airdrops of food and medicine would be carried out to help the local citizens. American and coalition soldiers would then go in on the ground to root out any remaining Taliban forces and al-Qaeda soldiers. The last stage would be to stabilize the region and help the people of Afghanistan to become a free society.

The United Nations and the United States asked that the Taliban turn over bin Laden for prosecution—or a war would commence. The Taliban offered to try him in an Islamic court, but the United States would not accept these propositions. On September 24, the Taliban called for a jihad against the United States if it sent military forces into Afghanistan. The United States knew it would be important to have support from other Muslim nations when the United States invaded. Saudi Arabia said that Afghan leaders were defaming Islam by supporting terrorists. Pakistan had recognized the Taliban government as legitimate, but General Pervez Musharraf, Pakistan's president, pledged support for US efforts to arrest bin Laden and appealed to his nation to give its support on September 16, 2001.

Another player that the United States wanted support from was Russia. Having cooperation in the neighboring countries of Uzbekistan and Tajikistan would help the efforts. The United States and Russia have had a complicated history of tensions and working together. Though Russia is a democracy in name, it lacks a true independent multiparty system. Russia was largely influenced by the power and personality of one man: Vladimir Putin. Despite differences, the United States and Russia have worked together in the past, and with a war to wage in Afghanistan, Bush needed Putin's help. When Bush first met Putin, he asked about a cross that his mother had blessed in Jerusalem and had given to him. Bush saw how important that cross was to Putin and Putin's reaction to his question won Bush over. He called Putin a man that America could trust. Bush said, "I looked the man in the eye. I found him to be very straightforward and trustworthy. [...] I was able to get a sense of his soul."[3]

After a call on September 22, Putin agreed to let the United States use Russian airspace, and he helped to get the cooperation of Uzbekistan and Tajikistan. He told his Russian generals to share their experiences from fighting in the region.

At the same time that plans were coming together to engage in battle, Bush wanted to think beyond the conflict. Once the Taliban was removed, the question would be:

Who would run the country? He assigned Colin Powell the task of coming up with a plan so Afghanistan would not fall back under a tyrannical regime.

Although he knew this was the right decision, Bush confided in his memoirs that it was not an easy one. He knew that many things could go wrong—civilians could suffer and terrorists might launch a retaliatory attack on the United States. Some people in Pakistan, for example, saw an attack on Afghanistan as an attack on Islam.

Bombing Begins

Secretary of Defense Donald Rumsfeld worked closely with Franks, and on October 7, 2001, American and British forces began intensive bombing of Afghanistan. France, Germany, Australia, and Canada provided logistical support and later on, troops as well. Aerial bombing targeted the Taliban military bases in Kabul, Kandahar, Jalalabad, Kunduz, and Mazar-e-Sharif. Bush was concerned for the average citizens, too, and he made sure that planes were airdropping food rations and relief supplies to civilians.

The politics behind bombing the Taliban were tricky because it could be seen as an attack against all Islam. In fact, the Taliban labeled it as such. Osama bin Laden released a statement on Arabic Al Jazeera television, calling all Muslim people to unite and fight against this attack on the entire Muslim world.

Operations went well during the first hours of the bombardment, Bush wrote. He said that within that short time British and American assaults destroyed the Taliban's small air defense system and several of the al-Qaeda training camps.

The war against the Taliban in Afghanistan began with steady bombing in the fall of 2001. Here, soldiers board a Chinook helicopter as part of the invasion.

It seemed that the Taliban would not be handing over bin Laden, but on October 14, 2001, the Taliban offered to deliver Osama bin Laden to a neutral country if the United States halted bombing and if the Taliban was given evidence of bin Laden's involvement in 9/11. The United States said that it didn't need to produce evidence and proceeded with the war.[4]

Bush was eager to get Special Forces troops on the ground as well. He was frustrated early on because these soldiers were stationed in Uzbekistan, and the mountains, freezing temperatures, and blinding snowstorms were making it impossible to get these fighters where they needed to be in Afghanistan. It took twelve days from the start of the military action to get the Special Forces in position.

About three weeks into the mission, some doubts about the war were coming up in the United States. The media and public were expressing some uncertainty. But Bush knew that they had to hold the course. In *Decision Points*, Bush reassured his National Security Council that they shouldn't give in to second-guessing or panic caused by the press. He told them: "We're going to stay confident and patient, cool and steady."[5]

In early November, the Special Forces, along with CIA officers and the United States' allies, began to get results. They were able to mount a successful siege on the Taliban stronghold of Mazar-e-Sharif. On November 12, just over a month since the campaign had begun, Operation Enduring Freedom was able to take the capital city of Kabul from the Taliban.

The day after the city was free from the Taliban, the *Guardian* newspaper reported children were flying kites in the streets. Men forced to grow beards were flocking to buy razors. Women revealed their faces. One Kabul woman interviewed said, "The Taliban gave women no rights, only the right to stay at home." At the moment, there was joy; the next step would be figuring out how to establish a fair and strong government to keep the peace.[6]

By early December, those fighting for Kandahar, the last Taliban-held city, fled or surrendered. Taliban leader Mullah Mohammed Omar went into hiding.

After US forces freed Kabul from the oppressive Taliban regime, Afghans came out of their homes to celebrate a newfound freedom—many taking to the hills to fly kites.

A Man on a Motorcycle Roars to Power

As the Taliban was driven from the towns and cities, the United States was looking for a way to help build a new government to lead the country. George Tenet, director of the CIA, reported that an anti-Taliban movement was growing under a Pashtun leader named Hamid Karzai.

Another Plane Crash Puts America on Edge

Fighting a war on terrorism and facing a fear of anthrax, Americans were on edge and wary in late 2001. On November 12, panic hit when American Airlines Flight 587 to the Dominican Republic, crashed, killing all 260 aboard as well as five people on the ground. Law enforcement officials doubted that terrorists brought down the jet. An article in the *Atlantic* said that the NTSB "concluded that American Airlines training methods were to blame for [First Officer Sten] Molin's use of the rudder, which they say stressed the vertical stabilizer fin with nearly two times the normal amount of load pressure." Although not ruled a terrorist act, the accident put America on edge once again.[7]

Karzai had been traveling the southern province of Urozgan with a small band of US Special Forces soldiers, often speeding from one location to another by motorcycle. Bush related the tale of how Karzai rode his motorcycle to Pakistan, where he rallied men to take Tarinkot, a small city near Kandahar.

Karzai was born in the village of Karz, near Kandahar, Afghanistan. As a young man he traveled to Pakistan to join Mujahideen fighters who were resisting the Soviet occupation. These Muslim warriors of the faith based their name on the word *jihad*, a struggle against unbelievers.

Hamid Karzai became the first leader of a free and democratic Afghanistan after the fall of the oppressive Taliban regime.

Karzai served as deputy foreign minister in the Mujahideen government, established in Kabul in 1992. There were many different competing groups in Afghanistan, and he believed a Grand Council needed to be established so the differences between the competing parties could be resolved peacefully. In 1999, his father, Abdul Ahad Karzai, who was mounting a resistance to the Taliban, was assassinated. Karzai had dedicated his life to pushing for a more tolerant and united Afghanistan.[8]

On December 5, 2001, Hamid Karzai was elected chairman of the Interim Administration of Afghanistan by participants at the UN-sponsored Bonn Conference. He then went on to become the president of the Islamic Republic of Afghanistan. On December 7, the sixtieth anniversary of the attacks on Pearl Harbor, the Taliban regime gave up its stronghold in Kandahar, after only sixty-one days of war in Afghanistan.[9]

Into the Labyrinth

Al-Qaeda fighters continued to hide out in Afghanistan's mountainous Tora Bora region, where they engaged in combat with anti-Taliban Afghan forces, backed by US Special Forces troops. The Taliban leader Mullah Mohammed Omar went into hiding rather than surrender. The Tora Bora region, with its extensive cave system, provided a hard-to-penetrate shield against attack. According to the *New York Times*, the very cave where bin Laden was hiding had originally been partially financed by the United States.[10] In the 1980s, Afghans had been fighting against a Soviet invasion. At that time, the United States was supporting the jihad against the Soviet Union. Bin Laden—

and Hamid Karzai—were among these religious soldiers engaged in this fight. As the son of a wealthy construction company owner in Saudi Arabia, bin Laden flew in bull-dozers and other heavy equipment to help build the tunnels, bunkers, and base camps.

In the *New York Times*, an Afghan officer explained why the caves were so important: "They're rugged, formidable and isolated," he said. "If you know them, you can come and go with ease. But if you don't, they're a labyrinth that you can't penetrate. They rise in some places to 14,000 feet, and for 10 years the Soviets pummeled them with every-thing they had, but to absolutely no avail. Another reason they're so important is their proximity to the border and to Pakistan—less than 20 miles away."[11]

The Battle of Tora Bora was fought between December 12 and 17, 2001, with anti-Taliban Afghan forces, backed by coalition forces troops.[12] The United States and the coalition found fighting in this region very difficult. The local military leaders reportedly did not like each other, the weather was bitter cold, and the terrain was very rough. And because it was the holy month of Ramadan, Muslim soldiers were fasting and wanting to spend more time with their families.

A major part of the mission in 2001 was to kill bin Laden. As Special Forces honed in on the location of bin Laden after he was heard on the radio, Afghan soldiers made a surprise announcement that they had negotiated a cease-fire. Coalition forces planned to move ahead anyway but met resistance from the Afghan troops helping them. After twelve hours of negotiation, the Afghan allies agreed to rejoin the push to capture bin Laden. As heavy bombing continued and ground troops pushed in, coalition forces picked up messages that bin Laden was growing desperate. When bin Laden's radio signals stopped, allied forces thought that he probably had been killed. Although unconfirmed, that was thought to be the case for a long time until a video emerged in October 2004 showing him to be alive and well. Although it was clear that bin Laden had escaped, coalition forces killed an estimated two hundred Taliban and al-Qaeda soldiers in Tora Bora.

Coalition forces attempt to root out Taliban fighters hiding in the network of caves in the mountainous Tora Bora region.

Operation Anaconda

While things were progressing in establishing a new government in Afghanistan, and major cities were now free of harsh dictatorial government, the war was not over. In March 2002, the coalition was receiving reports that the Taliban and al-Qaeda troops were regrouping.

The military focus was now to destroy the remaining Taliban and al-Qaeda forces that were hiding in this region along the eastern border with Pakistan. In March 2002, intelligence showed that al-Qaeda and the Taliban were gathering strength in the mountains and caves of the Shah-e-Kot (meaning "Place of the King") valley in eastern Afghanistan. With two thousand coalition forces sent in to carry out Operation Anaconda, this would be the largest ground assault since the Gulf War.

A report on the PBS show *Frontline* said that the operation did not start off well for the allied forces.[13] They had expected between 150 and 200 enemy fighters in the valley but the enemy strength was more than double by some estimates, ranging between 500 and 1,000 soldiers. Coalition commanders estimated Operation Anaconda would last about three days but it stretched on for two weeks. On March 4, heavy fire from small arms and rocket-propelled grenades hit two MH-47 Chinook helicopters. Eight US soldiers died and eighty-two were wounded in action, but when Operation Anaconda concluded, US and Canadian forces said they had killed hundreds of al-Qaeda troops and captured major stores of ammunition as well as vital intelligence information.[14]

Still, Afghan commanders said that many al-Qaeda and Taliban soldiers managed to flee the valley. By this point, about six months since the invasion of Afghanistan began, twenty-seven Americans had been killed—a small number in terms of war but still a precious cost. President Bush did not take the loss of life lightly. He wrote letters to the family members of every American who lost his or her life on the battlefield. By the end of his presidency he had written letters to almost five thousand families.

REBUILDING AFGHANISTAN

After driving out the Taliban from most of Afghanistan, the Bush administration brought education, health care, and women's rights to millions of citizens.

For all due purposes, al-Qaeda and the Taliban had been driven from Afghanistan, and now the process of building a peace-keeping force needed to begin. In May 2002, the UN Security Council voted to keep a multinational peacekeeping team in Kabul, the capital and largest city in Afghanistan, with a population of more than three and a half million. As the only Muslim country to contribute soldiers to the peace-keeping force, Turkey took over the International Security Assistance Force (ISAF).

When Bush had campaigned against Al Gore in 2000, he was wary about the United States using troops as nation builders, but Afghanistan became his nation-building mission. To bring the different tribes and people together, Bush and coalition forces respected Afghan tradition. In June 2002, a traditional council, or *loya jirga*, was assembled.[1] Representing districts throughout the country, about 1,500 delegates, including 160 women, gathered in Kabul. On the third day of the gathering Hamid Karzai was elected as interim president in a landslide of 1,295 votes.[2]

With the help of millions of dollars in American aid, Karzai and a new government began to rebuild Afghanistan. The money was used to rebuild roads and structures, train teachers, print textbooks, and deliver clean water and electricity to the population. Three million children soon returned to school. To keep the peace and prevent the Taliban from returning, America kept eight thousand troops stationed in the country along with five thousand soldiers from a coalition of twenty-two countries.

In July 2002, US planes dropped bombs on a village in Uruzgan Province, thinking they were targeting Taliban leaders, but they had made a mistake. They attacked people who were at a wedding and celebrating by shooting guns in the air. The air assault killed more than forty villagers. The incident put a strain on relations between America and Afghanistan, and it highlighted how civilians often became the innocent victims of war. The Watson Institute of International and Public Affairs at Brown University estimated that more than thirty-one thousand of those killed in Afghanistan since the war began in 2001 had been civilians.[3]

The Taliban would not slink away quietly. Terrorists committed several isolated attacks on new government officials. In February 2002, Abdul Rahman, the minister of civil aviation and tourism, was stabbed to death at the

Although the Taliban was no longer the ruling force in Afghanistan, its supporters kept up terrorist attacks, often destroying buildings and lives with explosive devices.

Kabul airport. Rebels tried to blow up the defense minister in April 2002. Two gunmen murdered the vice president in July, and Karzai himself narrowly escaped an assassination attempt on September 5.[4]

In 2006, the Taliban and al-Qaeda fighters continued to launch attacks on the new Afghan government, so NATO added more troops to the area. But the BBC reported that by the beginning of 2007, violence was spreading again. Suicide bombings were on the rise, as was the use of improvised explosive devices (IEDs).[5]

A Foundation for Democracy

Nearly half a million Afghan citizens joined in public meetings to decide on a new constitution, which was adopted in January 2004. The constitution backed equality for women. Later that year, eighteen candidates ran for president, and about ten and a half million citizens registered to vote. In October, Karzai became the president again with 55 percent of the vote.[6] A few weeks later, bin Laden suddenly reappeared on the Arab television network Al Jazeera. He taunted the Bush administration and took responsibility for the 9/11 attacks. He said, "We want to restore freedom to our nation, just as you lay waste to our nation."

Bin Laden would not, however, reclaim Afghanistan, and steps toward a stronger free government continued. The first-ever free, democratic parliamentary and provincial council elections in Afghanistan were held on September 18, 2005. The new National Assembly would have two chambers, a directly elected lower house, the Wolesi Jirga, and an upper house, the House of Elders, composed of appointed and indirectly elected candidates. These were the first peaceful nationwide elections in thirty years. After the election, the new National Assembly included sixty-eight women and representatives from almost every ethnic group, Bush wrote in his memoirs.[7]

In the more than a decade since this first election, Taliban and al-Qaeda forces have continued to push back against this fledgling democracy. An article in the *New York Times* on December 2, 2016, stated that forty thousand to forty-five thousand militants were active across Afghanistan and that the government controlled only about 60 percent of the country.[8] The Taliban still held control over

After the war, improving the infrastructure in the country was a major goal. Here, workers are seen paving a new road.

10 percent of Afghanistan. At the end of October 2016, scores of regular Afghan soldiers had surrendered to the Taliban, a trend the *New York Times* said was repeating in other provinces. That year, the Taliban had taken more territory in Afghanistan than at any time since 2002, according to United Nations data. At the same time, the Afghan military suffered a drop in numbers, according to data from the US military, and military casualty rates rose to a historic high. So as of this writing, while a democratic government is in place, extremists have been pushing back and threatening the stability of the region.

As early as 2005, Bush recognized that these types of difficulties might lie ahead. He wrote about the problems of coordinating military forces and training a sustainable Afghan army. Opium production was booming in southern Afghanistan. Corruption was diverting funds from the central government as warlords in different regions took customs collections for themselves.

The Pakistan Problem

Bush also saw that a lot of the trouble was arising out of Pakistan. Reports had shown that al-Qaeda and Taliban forces were fleeing and regrouping in eastern Pakistan. Bush worked closely with President Pervez Musharraf to round up suspected terrorists in Pakistan.[9] As Pakistan turned over more suspected terrorists to the United States, Bush lifted sanctions and sent the country more economic aid. Musharraf agreed to give the United States access to three airbases to launch its attacks on the Taliban. Still, the relationship between Pakistan and the United States remains complicated, and terrorists have continued to take refuge in tribal regions.

Rather than focusing on terrorism, Pakistan's military often concentrated its efforts on disputes with India, which have existed since 1947. In this year, Britain left the region called British India, which it had occupied for three hundred years. Before doing so, Britain divided the country into the Hindu-majority India and the Muslim-majority Pakistan. The partitioning led to horrifying outbreaks of violence. Since August 1947, India and Pakistan have fought three major wars and one minor war over territorial disputes. The boundary line in Jammu and Kashmir is particularly disputed.

Pakistan's president, Pervez Musharraf, pledged his support to round up Taliban and al-Qaeda terrorists who found refuge in Pakistan but his efforts were often half-hearted.

Both Pakistan and India have nuclear weapons, and both India and the United States have condemned Pakistan for harboring terrorists. In fact, when Osama bin Laden was eventually tracked down and killed under President Obama on May 2, 2011, he was found in a large compound in Abottobad, Pakistan. In 2006, Bush kept up the pressure on Musharraf to keep extremists from hiding in Pakistan, but it seemed clear that Taliban and al-Qaeda forces were still able to hide within the country. Karzai was furious with Musharraf.

Bush brought the two to a dinner at the White House in September 2006. Although the meal was tense, the

Guantanamo Bay:
A Controversial Prison

As the war against terrorism, al-Qaeda, and the Taliban progressed, the coalition forces began capturing prisoners. These captives presented the question, where do you put captured enemy combatants and how should their detention be handled? For this purpose, the United States established a detention camp at Guantanamo Bay, a US naval base located on the southern coast of Cuba. The United States operated the base in Cuba because of a long-standing lease that dates back to the Spanish-American War. The prison camp, which gained the nickname "Gitmo," was established in January 2002 to detain extraordinarily dangerous

In 2002, George W. Bush established Guantanamo Bay detention camp in Cuba as a US military prison to hold detainees captured during the war on terror.

people, to interrogate detainees in an optimal setting, and to prosecute detainees.

Prisoners here, however, could be held indefinitely without trial by a US court or international body. The Geneva Conventions is a body of public international law designed to protect prisoners of war and wounded and sick soldiers during wartime; their purpose has been to make the effects of war more tolerable for civilians and soldiers. The conventions established that prisoners must be treated humanely. Bush's Justice Department wrote that al-Qaeda and Taliban prisoners did not have these rights because they were not legitimate entities protected under international war laws. The treatment and rights of these prisoners caused division within the Bush administration. Some within the administration said that the war on terrorism was radically different from other wars, so the same rules did not apply. Bush promised to treat prisoners humanely.

In the spring of 2002, the question came up of how these prisoners could be interrogated if it was thought they had information vital to US security. When the CIA captured a high-level al-Qaeda member in Pakistan named Khalid Sheikh Mohammed, they thought that he was holding back important information. Bush ultimately approved some controversial techniques for interrogations including sleep deprivation, slapping, and "waterboarding," a type of torture where water is poured over a captive's face until he feels like he is drowning. The Justice Department turned down one CIA approach it wanted to use—burying a person alive until the point of suffocation. Using waterboarding, the CIA was able to get important information from Mohammed. He reportedly was waterboarded 183 times.[10]

two finally agreed to share more intelligence and work with tribes along their shared border to promote peace.[11] But Musharraf could not control the tribes and terrorists flowing into Afghanistan. He served as both army chief and head of state, a conflict that many in his country thought violated the law. He eventually resigned from the military on November 28, 2007, which helped relieve some political pressure. Ultimately, however, the country saw that Musharraf was eroding trust in the nation, and he resigned as leader of the nation on August 18, 2008. But with all this instability, terrorists were able to increase their operations and heighten their assaults in Afghanistan.

Peacekeeping efforts continue to this day in Afghanistan. About 8,400 troops were stationed in Afghanistan at the end of 2016, but that is far less than the 40,000 who were there at the end of George W. Bush's term.[12] In the month before he left office, Bush paid a farewell visit to the troops in Afghanistan to thank all the soldiers who served the country. He told a hangar full of troops: "Thanks for making the noble choice to serve and protect your fellow Americans. What you're doing in Afghanistan is important, it is courageous, and it is selfless. It's akin to what American troops did in places like Normandy and Iwo Jima and Korea. Your generation is every bit as great as any that has come before. And the work you do every day is shaping history for generations to come."

Bush left office proud that free elections were being held, millions of children were in school, and health care was available to 80 percent of the population. But the challenges of poverty and extremist influences continue.

CHAPTER FIVE

A PIVOT TO IRAQ

Bush depended on the support of England and Prime Minister Tony Blair going into the Iraq war: "As the years passed and the wartime decisions grew tougher, some of our allies wavered. Tony Blair never did."

For George W. Bush and his administration, the war on terrorism did not begin and end with Afghanistan. The focus on Iraq as a source of turmoil in the Middle East continued.

Since the first Persian Gulf War ended in 1991 and Bush's father left Saddam Hussein in power, the dictator had ruled with his Ba'ath Party. The Ba'ath Party's objectives were secularism, socialism, and pan-Arab unionism. The Ba'ath Party was also strong in Syria, where Bashar al-Assad had been the president of the country since July 2000, but he was also the general secretary of the Arab Socialist Ba'ath Party. In Iraq, Saddam Hussein and his Ba'ath Party assumed the presidency in 1979 and ruled

Saddam Hussein and the Ba'ath Party ruled Iraq for twenty-four years. During that time, Iraq was notorious for human rights violations and political oppression.

the country for twenty-four years. Saddam dreamed of an Arab empire spanning the Middle East—a new Ottoman Empire ruled by Arabs.

Originally, the United States had backed Saddam when Iraq went to war against Iran from 1980 to 1988, seeing his dictatorship as a means to maintain stability in the region and as a connection to its vast oil supplies. The United States even gave Iraq arms, money, and satellite intelligence, as well as chemical and biological-weapon precursors, according to the Global Policy Forum.[1]

Much of the strife in Iraq arises from two major branches of the Muslim religion: Sunni and Shia. The Shiites are in the majority in Iraq, making up about two-thirds of the population, while the Sunnis comprise about 20 percent. Iraq is only one of a few countries with a Shiite majority according to the Pew Research Center.[2]

Iraq Was Once a Diverse Land

Centuries ago, the region that is now Iraq was much more diverse. For ages, Jews lived and thrived in Babylon, located in modern-day Iraq. The Jewish community in Baghdad numbered about 140,000 in 1940 but has dropped to practically zero today.[3] In 2011, WikiLeaks claimed there were just seven Jews living there. The Christian population in Iraq was at more than one million in 2003 and was estimated at less than three hundred thousand by 2014.

Saddam claimed to be a secular dictator, but he was born Sunni and he treated the Shiite majority brutally.

The Formation of ISIS

Note that after Saddam's government was eventually toppled, the differences and animosities between Shia and Sunnis led to more unrest in the region.[4] With Saddam out of power, a series of coalition governments were formed with the Shia party dominating, but that led to Sunni unrest. The United States decided to rid the military and civil services of thousands of Sunnis who had been loyal to Saddam. These Sunnis were now without jobs.

As Iraq excluded more Sunnis from the government and gave Shiites disproportionate benefits, a militant Sunni movement called the Islamic State (IS) rose. The group began to take over large swaths of land in Iraq and Syria. When it captured Mosul in 2014, the group had taken the name of the Islamic State of Iraq and Syria or ISIS. It declared itself a caliphate, a political-religious state comprising the Muslim community and the lands and peoples under its dominion. As a statement in the *Week* said, it should be noted that ISIS is a radical Islamic group/movement, but it does not, by any means, represent the views of the vast majority of Muslims.[5] ISIS conducted a war of terrorism and brutality. For example, ISIS beheaded many of its prisoners, including US journalist James Foley, and tried to instill terror by putting videos of these brutal actions online. Insurgents in Afghanistan, Pakistan, Nigeria, Indonesia, Egypt, Bangladesh, Philippines, Saudi Arabia, and Yemen pledged allegiance to ISIS. Groups in these areas flew the black flag of this terrorist group.

In its short history, ISIS has launched at least 143 attacks in 29 countries, killing 2,043 people since declaring itself a caliphate. One of the most severe attacks took place in Paris on November 13, 2015, when ISIS claimed responsibility for coordinated assaults that took the lives of 130 people, including 89 who were gunned down at the Bataclan concert hall while attending a show by the US band the Eagles of Death Metal. In San Bernadino, California, on December 2, 2015, Tashfeen Malik and her husband, Syed Rizwan Farook, shot 14 people to death and injured 21 others at a gathering of local government health workers. They were later gunned down in a shootout with law enforcement. It appeared they were self-radicalized followers of ISIS. Malik had pledged allegiance to ISIS online, and the attack was labeled as ISIS-inspired.

On the morning of March 22, 2016, three coordinated suicide bombings occurred in Belgium killing thirty-two and injuring more than three hundred. ISIS has been very much like the Taliban in its severe control of its people— they have promoted slavery, rape, and genocide, killing many groups of people, including Christians, Alawites, and other Shiites and Yazidis. As of the end of 2016, five thousand US troops were supporting about forty thousand Iraqi soldiers in the fight to take back Mosul and defeat ISIS.[6]

Saddam's Continued Threat

After the first Persian Gulf War ended, the United States and allies set up a safe haven in northern Iraq for Kurds continually persecuted by Saddam's regime. The allies created "no-fly" zones where Iraqi aircraft could not travel. The United Nations established economic restrictions on

Iraq, partially to help prevent the country from developing any weapons of mass destruction. The United States was on the alert for any terrorist groups or unstable countries that might acquire nuclear, biological, or chemical weapons.

In his State of the Union address on January 29, 2002, Bush singled out three countries as the axis of evil: Iran, Iraq, and North Korea. For 2002, however, the United States and allies were focused on the fight in Afghanistan. Still, the administration saw Iraq as a particularly persistent danger while under the rule of Saddam. From the 1990s onward, the United Nations also had a close eye on Iraq, which they thought was making dangerous armaments.

The United Nations discovered a variety of forbidden weapons and technology in Iraq, and the country continually interfered with weapons inspections. As a result, President Bill Clinton ordered the bombing of Iraqi military bases in 1998 in Operation Desert Fox. Clinton made a primetime address saying, "The hard fact is that so long as Saddam remains in power, he threatens the well-being of his people, the peace of his region, the security of the world. The best way to end that threat once and for all is with a new Iraqi government—a government ready to live in peace with its neighbors, a government that respects the rights of its people."[7] While Iraq kept putting off inspectors, neighboring countries reopened trade with the country.[8]

Turning Up the Heat

Bush had been strengthening his alliance with Britain throughout the war in Afghanistan, and in February 2001 he invited Prime Minister Tony Blair and his wife, Cherie, to the United States for a visit. He said that he knew the

British prime minister Tony Blair became a steadfast ally of George Bush's in both the wars in Afghanistan and Iraq.

Bushes and the Blairs would get along because when they were choosing a movie to watch after dinner, "they agreed on *Meet the Parents*, a comedy starring Robert De Niro and Ben Stiller." In Tony Blair, Bush found a strong ally who considered Saddam a threat to the world.

On the other hand, Bush found that Russia and France had economic interests in Iraq and did not want to go to war. Russia had extensive oil contracts, and Bush wrote that "Vladimir Putin didn't consider Saddam a threat." Jacques Chirac of France supported aggressive inspections but was wary of military force. Bush in his biography also complained that he felt his trust was betrayed by German chancellor Gerhard Schroeder, who said he would back Bush's attack on Iraq but later denounced the use of force.

Just before the start of the New Year in 2002, Bush and General Tommy Franks met regularly to plan strategy for a possible invasion. Bush wanted to do his utmost to protect civilians from violence and starvation. He wanted to protect allied troops from any possible attack from biological or chemical weapons. On August 5, 2002, Bush said that Tommy Franks had a plan to massively bomb military sites and then swiftly take over WMD (weapons of mass destruction) sites, Iraq's southern oil fields, and Scud missile launchers. Scud missiles were originally Soviet-designed, and their principal threat was that the warheads had potential to hold chemical or biological agents. Franks told Bush that the operation was going to rely on "shock and awe," a term that was often used to describe the initial assault on Iraq.[9]

Bush had gotten reports in the summer of 2002 that Abu Musab al-Zarqawi, a terrorist connected with al-Qaeda, might be operating a lab in northeastern Iraq to develop biological weapons using ricin and cyanide. He would later go on to be a founder of ISIS. The CIA worked together with Arab intelligence to get Saddam to extradite al-Zarqawi, but he refused to act. The Pentagon drafted plans to attack the camp with cruise missiles and airstrikes, but these were not acted upon. Some said that while military officials had an airtight case for attacking al-Zarqawi's operation, the administration feared destroying the terrorist camp in Iraq could undercut its case for war against Saddam. Bush in his biography said that he was concerned that an attack would cause "an international firestorm," and that this would get in the way of actions to build a united force to fight Saddam.

The Hunt for Weapons of Mass Destruction

In 2002, Bush encouraged allies to pressure Saddam to reveal any development of weapons of mass destruction. Bush and his administration were convinced that Iraq had such weapons, although these accusations were later proven false. But Saddam had a long history of defying UN resolutions—not complying with sixteen of them dating back to the Gulf War. After two years of searching 1,700 sites in Iraq, carried out by 1,625 UN and US inspectors at a cost of more than $1 billion, CIA's Iraq Survey Group (ISG) concluded that Saddam had ambitions to restart at least some chemical and nuclear programs once sanctions were lifted, according to an article in the *Guardian*. However, he had destroyed his last weapons of mass destruction more than a decade before, and his capacity to build new ones had been dwindling for years by the time the United States and coalition forces did invade.[10]

On June 1, 2002, Bush told the graduating class at West Point that the United States must be prepared to take preemptive action to stop any potential attacks. Throughout this year, Bush was building a case for military action against Iraq, and behind the scenes he was drawing up battle plans for an invasion of the country. Some in his administration tried to directly connect Saddam to al-Qaeda and 9/11, but Bush pushed that reasoning aside.

James Mann in his biography on the president said that Bush was more likely embracing the idea that Saddam was an oppressive dictator who had abused human rights and freedoms and should be deposed.[11] Bush wrote that Saddam and his henchman "had tortured innocent people, raped political opponents in front of their families, scalded dissidents with acid, and dumped tens of thousands of Iraqis into mass graves." Saddam had used horrible mustard gas and nerve gas when fighting against Iran from 1980 to 1988. In 1988, Saddam's regime also used deadly chemicals, massacring more than five thousand Kurdish civilians in the village of Halabja.

While certain groups favored the policy of preemptive war, many were opposed. In August, an editorial piece was published in the conservative *Wall Street Journal* with the headline, "Don't Attack Saddam."[12]

In September, Bush gathered his national security team. Vice President Dick Cheney suggested that the case against Saddam had to be restated. Then he should be given one to two months to reveal all. If he couldn't show complete compliance with disarming, the United States would be forced to act. Colin Powell argued for UN involvement to make sure the United States had international support. Bush decided to seek a UN resolution before acting. He also met with Tony Blair to make sure he had his backing, and Blair assured him that he agreed with the strategy. Bush told one of Blair's top aides: "Your man has got cojones."[13]

A SHORT WAR BUT A LINGERING BATTLE

Bush was surprised to learn that intelligence had been wrong and there were no weapons of mass destruction. "If Saddam doesn't actually have WMD, I asked myself, why on earth would he subject himself to a war he will almost certainly lose."

In October 2002, Bush asked for and received a congressional vote authorizing the use of force against Saddam Hussein. Even leading Democrats such as senators Joe Biden, John Kerry, and Hillary Clinton voted in favor of the attack. In this political climate, many saw a vote against military action as weak or even unpatriotic.

Colin Powell then mounted negotiations to get the United Nations to pass a resolution that would allow the United States to take action against Iraq. On November 8, 2002, the UN Security Council passed Resolution 1441, demanding that Iraq readmit inspectors. France, Germany, Russia, Syria, and China supported this provision that Iraq be given a final opportunity to divulge any program to develop weapons of mass destruction and then to disarm them. If Saddam resisted, it was clear that there would be "serious consequences."[1] Saddam had the opportunity to reveal all and also to simply step aside and reside in exile in a neighboring country with his sons. But he refused.

In December, Iraq handed over a twelve-thousand-page weapons declaration as required by the United Nations.[2] The document was meant to be a current and complete

US secretary of state Colin Powell made a presentation before the United Nations to convince the world that Iraq was deliberately hiding weapons of mass destruction.

account of all Iraq's chemical, biological, nuclear, and missile programs, but UN inspectors said that the Iraqi arms declaration contained little new information about its weapons of mass destruction capability.

By the end of 2002, Bush had built up the military in Kuwait and at other locations near Iraq. Some thought that this show of power would convince Saddam to back down. In early 2003, police in London arrested six terror suspects who were thought to have ricin (one of the world's deadliest poisons) and discovered a ricin lab connected to the camp in Iraq.[3] That month, Tony Blair, the prime minister of England, joined Bush in declaring that Saddam Hussein was continuing to block UN inspections and that the country had dangerous weapons.

Shortly after the new year of 2003, the United States was making the motions and preparations for war, but Bush knew the costs of war in money and lives, and he still hoped to avoid it. He wrote a letter to his daughters who were in college: "I am working hard to keep the peace and avoid war. I pray that the man in Iraq will disarm in a peaceful way. We are putting pressure on him to do just that and much of the world is with us."[4]

Toward the end of January, the UN's chief weapons inspector, Hans Blix, told the United Nations that there were "many unanswered questions" about Iraq's weapons programs, but inspectors had not "found any smoking guns" that might trigger war.[5] A couple of weeks later they found twelve warheads designed to carry chemical weapons. The inspectors believed the warheads had not been accounted for in Iraq's twelve-thousand-page submission. Blix said, "Iraq appears not to have come to a genuine acceptance, not even today, of the disarmament that was demanded of it.[6]

While some nations believed that the inspectors needed more time to investigate matters in Iraq, Britain and the United States seized upon this latest information that Iraq was being dishonest and not disarming. In his State of the Union address on January 28, 2003, Bush told the nation that the United States was now ready to go to war, even without a mandate from the United Nations.[7] Bush later admitted that Saddam had no weapons of mass destruction, but he believed Iraq had the capacity to make those weapons. In *Decision Points*, Bush wrote: "In retrospect, of course, we all should have pushed harder on the intelligence and revisited our assumptions. But at the same time, the evidence and logic pointed in the other direction. If Saddam doesn't actually have WMD, I asked myself, why on earth would he subject himself to a war he will almost certainly lose?"[8]

Tony Blair wanted to get another UN resolution, making it clear that Iraq had failed to be open and transparent about its weapons. Iraq had not taken its final opportunity to avoid war. Colin Powell made the case before the UN Security Council, saying: "The facts on Iraq's behavior demonstrate that Saddam Hussein and his regime have made no effort—no effort—to disarm as required by the international community. Indeed, the facts and Iraq's behavior show that Saddam Hussein and his regime are concealing efforts to produce more weapons of mass destruction."[9]

As Bush later wrote, many of Powell's assertions would turn out to be inaccurate, but at the time they were based on known intelligence. At the root of wanting to remove Saddam, however, was still the fact that he was a ruthless dictator. Bush sought out many sources for advice as he was deciding on his course of action. One voice that swayed him was that of Holocaust survivor and founding chairman of the United States Holocaust Memorial Council Elie Wiesel, who told Bush, "Mr. President, you have a moral obligation to act against evil."[10]

As with the war in Afghanistan, Bush was also concerned about civilians in the region as plans for invasion moved ahead. Staff drew up strategies to deliver food, blankets, medicine, tents, and other relief supplies. Bush wanted to ensure that international organizations that specialized in relief would be at the ready to come in and help with sheltering and feeding refugees. He and his team designed plans for nation building, such as long-term reconstruction, building hospitals, and calling for Iraqi doctors and nurses living abroad to return and help their newly freed nation. Bush and his team made plans to hold elections. Bush felt strongly that the Iraqis needed to pick their own leaders.

Again, while many supported the move toward war, many opposed it. An article in *Time* magazine stated that on February 15, 2003, the world saw one of the largest single coordinated protests in history—about ten million to fifteen million people assembled and marched in more than six hundred cities to voice their opposition to a war in Iraq. As many as three million flooded the streets of Rome; more than a million gathered in London and Barcelona; and approximately two hundred thosusand rallied in San Francisco and in New York City.[11]

Still, the momentum was now toward war with Iraq, and on February 24, the United States, Great Britain, and Spain submitted a proposed resolution to the UN Security Council stating that Iraq had failed to take the final opportunity to stop an invasion. About a week later, however, France, Russia, and Germany released a joint statement saying that they would not support UN authorization of military action in Iraq. Mexico and Chile refused to vote at all. Iraq then promised to accelerate inspections. But on March 16, Spain, the United States, and Britain demanded the immediate disarmament of Iraq.

On March 17, George Bush addressed the American people. He said, "My fellow citizens. Events in Iraq have now reached the final days of decision. For more than a decade, the United States and other nations have pursued patient and honorable efforts to disarm the Iraqi regime without war. That regime pledged to reveal and destroy all its weapons of mass destruction as a condition for ending the Persian Gulf War in 1991. Since then the world has engaged in 12 years of diplomacy. We have passed more than a dozen resolutions in the United Nations Security Council. We have sent hundreds of weapons inspectors to oversee the disarmament of Iraq. Our good faith has not been returned. The Iraqi regime has used diplomacy as a ploy to gain time and advantage. It has uniformly defied Security Council resolutions demanding full disarmament."

He went on to say: "Intelligence gathered by this and other governments leaves no doubt that the Iraq regime continues to possess and conceal some of the most lethal weapons ever devised. This regime has already used weapons of mass destruction against Iraq's neighbors and

Freedom Fries

In 2003, when France opposed going to war in Iraq, the House of Representatives' cafeterias stopped serving "French" fries, renaming them "freedom fries."

against Iraq's people … Before the day of horror can come, before it is too late to act, this danger will be removed.

"We are now acting because the risks of inaction would be far greater. In one year, or five years, the power of Iraq to inflict harm on all free nations would be multiplied many times over. Free nations have a duty to defend our people by uniting against the violent, and tonight, as we have done before, America and our allies accept that responsibility."[12]

On March 18, Bush got the further support from Britain that he had hoped for. Elected members of the British Parliament gave approval for the invasion of Iraq in a series of two votes, on March 18, 2003.

He gave Saddam one last chance to avoid conflict, saying that he and his sons must leave Iraq within forty-eight hours or military conflict would commence.

Bush also made one last zero-hour attempt to avoid war by trying to kill Saddam in a bombing attack of a compound near Baghdad, the capital of Iraq. The CIA had a tip that Saddam was staying there, but the intelligence was wrong.

In March, the United States put its forces in place: Operation Iraqi Freedom would launch with a coalition of about 160,000 troops from the United States, the United Kingdom, Poland, and Australia.

On March 20, President Bush declared that the war, dubbed Operation Iraqi Freedom, had begun.[13] The first bombing attacks were directed at an installation where Saddam was believed to be meeting. An overall strategy was to try to get Saddam Hussein at all costs. Deputy Defense Secretary Paul Wolfowitz said that bringing down Saddam was essential to topple the regime. "It's almost like cutting off the head of the snake, and the rest of the body will go," he said.[14] Bush said, "We have no ambition in Iraq, except to remove a threat and restore control of that country to its own people."[15]

Air forces bombarded the capital as forces on the ground crossed into Iraq's southern border from Kuwait.

March 20, 2003, marked the start of the war against Iraq. American troops off-loaded in Kuwait as Operation Iraqi Freedom was just beginning.

Bush said that the bomb attacks were precisely targeted with a goal to spare the civilian population and infrastructure. While Germany did not support the war, it did allow American troops to fly over its territory. Turkey, however, was more problematic. The NATO ally would not open up its airspace or allow US aircraft to refuel there.

Coalition forces swiftly took over key oil fields and liberated the southern city of Basra and the port of Umm Qasr. The Zarqawi camp was targeted and destroyed with help from Kurdish forces. As the second week of the invasion came to a close, after enduring sandstorms and severe heat, the troops had reached the city limits of

Baghdad. The soldiers were also weighed down by heavy HAZMAT outfits to protect them from any possible biological or chemical assaults. Although Saddam's loyal forces fought back from civilian vehicles and often used civilians as shields, the coalition forces advanced in armored vehicles, pushed back Saddam's men, and handed out candy and medicine to civilians as they moved forward.

On April 4, CNN reported that explosions were rocking the capital one after another for minutes on end. CNN said that Iraqis tried to stop the US advance by charging with dump trucks, pickup trucks, and buses filled with Iraqi soldiers firing their weapons.

US military forces used a "shock and awe" campaign to fight Iraq, bombarding the capital of Baghdad in heavy, unrelenting missile fire.

Just twenty days after Operation Iraqi Freedom began, American troops took over Baghdad and toppled a huge statue of Saddam Hussein as crowds cheered.

A Dramatic Act of Bravery

In *Military Times,* a story recalled how Sergeant Paul Ray Smith set up a temporary enemy prisoner-of-war holding area during the seizure of Saddam International Airport when his unit came under attack. "Smith kept his soldiers focused during the fight while engaging the Iraqi force of around 100 men with his M16, a hand grenade and an AT4 anti-armor weapon. At one point in the battle, Smith manned a .50 caliber machine gun in the exposed turret of a damaged M113 armored personnel carrier and began firing at the main force of the enemy. He fired about 400 rounds, giving his soldiers time to regroup and mount an attack of their own. When the shooting stopped, the Iraqi force had been defeated, but not before Smith had suffered an enemy bullet to the head."[16]

Just twenty days after the invasion began on April 9, US troops and allies took over Baghdad. On TV, Iraqis danced and waved the country's pre-1991 flag in central Baghdad's Firdos Square, after a US Marine armored recovery vehicle helped topple the square's huge statue of Saddam Hussein. Other Iraqis were tearing down portraits of Saddam Hussein and throwing shoes—a serious insult in the Arab world.

MISSION ACCOMPLISHED?:
THE POST-WAR BLUES

Bush would come to regret standing in front of a banner reading "Mission Accomplished" in 2003. Although the initial invasion of Iraq was a success, much bloodshed and unrest was yet to come.

On May 1, 2003, Bush decided to give a speech on board the USS *Abraham Lincoln*, an aircraft carrier with about five thousand sailors, airmen, and marines on board who were returning home after months of supporting efforts in Afghanistan and Iraq. Although Saddam was not yet captured, operations in taking over Iraq were going relatively smoothly, so Bush planned to make a speech to announce that major combat was over and that a new phase of the war had begun. In his speech, he said, "My fellow Americans, major combat operations in Iraq have ended ... The transition from dictatorship to democracy will take time, but it is worth every effort. Our coalition will stay until our work is done. Then we will leave, and we will leave behind a free Iraq."[1]

Lined up behind him for television cameras was a huge banner reading "Mission Accomplished." Bush admitted in his memoirs that this turned out to be a huge mistake. He said that it became shorthand criticism for all that subsequently went wrong in Iraq.

Controlling the Aftermath of War

One factor that Bush did not anticipate was the lawlessness that broke out weeks after the Iraqi people were liberated. Kidnappings, murders, rapes, and lootings were reported. Thieves had plundered an estimated fifteen thousand items

While giving his "Mission Accomplished" speech, President Bush told the nation that major fighting was over. In reality, the fighting and death toll had just begun.

from Baghdad's Iraq Museum, including ritual vessels, heads from sculptures, amulets, Assyrian ivories, and more than five thousand cylinder seals, according to *Smithsonian Magazine*.[2] Since the war, many of the valuables have been retrieved. Bush wrote that there was a security and political vacuum in the city.

To get the country back on its feet and organized for the future, Bush put counterterrorism expert Paul Bremer, former ambassador, in charge of developing a legitimate government in May, and the UN Security Council backed this US-led administration in Iraq. Bremer would oversee the Coalition Provisional Authority, which would help keep order in Iraq while the Iraqi people drafted a constitution and established elections. In July 2016, Bremer wrote in the *Guardian*: "When I arrived in Baghdad, all of the Iraqi government ministries had been looted. Some were still afire. We had about 40,000 coalition forces in the capital, but their very restrictive rules of engagement did not allow them to use force to stop the looting."[3]

Among Bremer's first orders as the head of the Coalition Provisional Authority was to abolish ministries and institutions that formed the backbone of Saddam's power structure. He also banned members of the Ba'ath Party from holding public office and disbanded the Iraqi army. Some critics now say this was a mistake because out-of-work Sunni warriors forged alliances with a Sunni insurgency that would eventually grow to become the Islamic State of Iraq and Syria (ISIS). Many former Iraqi military officers and troops, trained under Saddam, have spent years in Anbar Province battling both US troops and Baghdad's

Shiite-dominated security forces, according to an article in *Time* magazine.[4]

In his memoir, Bush recognized the problem the United States had helped create. The majority of the population was Shia and Kurds, and they wanted a clean break from Saddam, so keeping Saddam's Ba'ath Party members out of government and the military seemed to make sense at the time. However, when many ex-Ba'ath Party members and Sunnis did not see a place for them in the new Iraqi government, they joined the insurgency and formed an alliance with ISIS. [5]

Bush criticized Ahmed Chalabi, who was appointed by the Shia-led government to chair the de-Ba'athification commission. In his obituary in the *Guardian*, it said that Chalabi used his position to purge hundreds of Sunni politicians who wanted to run for parliament thereby "paving the way for the sectarian polarization that provoked the emergence of the extremist Sunni group Islamic State."[6]

"Bring 'em on!": Attacks Escalate

During the summer of 2003, attacks from extremists escalated. In July, a reporter interviewed Bush about the attacks on the troops, and he replied that if anyone thought these attacks would make us leave early, to "bring 'em on!" He thought that comment would show confidence, but to some the remark was cocky and irresponsible. In their eyes, it made light of troop deaths and had the potential to provoke Iraqi insurgents and escalate the violence even further, which would lead to even more deaths among American troops.

Mid-July also brought together for the first time twenty-five Iraqis appointed by US and British officials to form Iraq's interim governing council.

One dramatic violent incident happened in August 2003, when a suicide bomber drove a cement mixer full of explosives into the side of the United Nations compound in Baghdad. The explosion killed seventeen people and wounded about one hundred. The *New York Times* reported: "The suicide bombing marked a brazen assault on the American occupation here, apparently calculated to destroy any sense of security for people charged with reviving Iraq in the aftermath of the war. If anarchy was the goal today, it was anarchy that unfolded."[7] Other attacks included roadside bombs and kidnappings of construction workers. One of the deadliest attacks since the regime of Saddam Hussein fell came on August 30, 2003, when a massive car bomb exploded outside the Imam Ali Mosque, claiming the lives of Shiite Islam's top clerics and 124 others.[8]

Many in the press and in the world were also asking about the absence of weapons of mass destruction. Bush, too, was surprised. The WMDs never materialized. He wrote in his memoir that he was stung by a mantra from the left: "Bush lied, people died." But he said that was wrong. He and his administration had not lied; they were simply wrong. Still, he stood by the rationale for invading Iraq: Saddam was a threat. He wrote, "No one was more shocked or angry than I was when we didn't find the weapons. I had a sickening feeling every time I thought about it. I still do."[9] (Ultimately, on March 31, 2005, the Commission on the Intelligence Capabilities of the United States Regarding Weapons of Mass Destruction reported that the intelligence community was "dead wrong" in its assessments of Iraq's weapons of mass destruction capabilities before the US invasion.)

On July 22, 2003, former Iraqi dictator Saddam Hussein's sons, Qusay and Uday Hussein, were killed after a three-hour firefight with US forces in the northern Iraqi city of Mosul. The two men had a reputation for being even more cruel and ruthless than their father, and many Iraqis celebrated their death. President Bush learned that Saddam Hussein ordered the deaths of Bush's daughters in retribution for the death of his sons, but these were nothing but idle threats.

After nine months of searching, US soldiers finally captured Saddam Hussein, who was hiding in a hole about 8 feet (2.4 meters) deep, a few miles outside of his hometown of Tikrit. He was dirty with matted hair and a bushy beard. He did not put up a fight, and one soldier described him as a man resigned to his fate. He was put in Iraqi custody and would face charges before a tribunal in the fall of 2005.

Were More Troops Needed?

While capturing Saddam was a relief, Bush knew that stabilizing the country would be a challenge. He wrote in his memoirs that he regretted cutting troop levels from 192,000 to 109,000 ten months following the invasion.[10] He did not want the United States to cause resentment by looking like occupiers. Bush wrote that the focus was on training Iraqis, but security should have been more of a priority. In looking back, it seemed the United States did not have enough troops to keep things calm. Ultimately, Bush wrote in his memoir that he still believed an Iraq led by Saddam Hussein would have made the world much less safe.

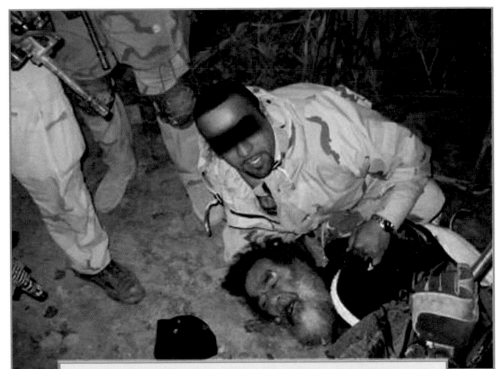

On December 13, 2003, US troops captured Saddam Hussein. They found him dirty and unshaven, hiding in an eight-foot hole near his hometown of Tikrit.

Steps Toward Independence

Throughout 2004, the United States proceeded with steps toward stabilizing Iraq and putting a new government in place. At the end of June, Paul Bremer, who was heading the Coalition Provisional Authority, restored formal sovereignty to Iraq in a simple meeting deep inside the heavily fortified area known as the Green Zone. The Coalition Authority was now dissolved. The US-appointed Iraqi Governing Council voted unanimously to endorse British-educated neurosurgeon Ayad Allawi as temporary prime minister.

The Shame of Abu Ghraib

Another challenge of the war was dealing with prisoners who fought for Saddam Hussein or who were extremists. Thousands of prisoners were held at Abu Ghraib prison, a US Army detention center. In the fall of 2003, photos were taken of naked Iraqi detainees being humiliated, and in the early half of 2004, those photos were made public. In May, Bush expressed his disgust with the mistreatment of Iraqi detainees. He told King Abdullah II of Jordan that he was "sorry for the humiliation suffered" by Iraqi prisoners at the hands of US troops. Bush vowed that any soldier found to be at fault would be punished.

At the beginning of September 2006, control of the Abu Ghraib Detention Facility was handed over to the Iraqis. CNN reported that the Iraqis made major renovations to Abu Ghraib to make it more humane, including building a new gym, barber shop, sewing room, outdoor recreational areas, a library, and computer room. The name was changed to Baghdad Central Prison.[11] But in 2014, the Iraqi government closed the prison because of fears that it might be overrun by Sunni insurgents who had been gaining strength.

Dr. Allawi vowed "a national unity and tolerance and brotherly behavior and spirit of peace and prosperity will prevail."[12] At this point, 850 servicemen and women had died, and Bush expressed hope that the transfer of formal sovereignty would undercut the insurgents' hopes of rallying the Iraqi people.

In the months prior to this transfer of power, insurgents were fighting back with a vengeance. Shia militias loyal to radical cleric Muqtada al-Sadr were battling coalition forces. Reportedly hundreds were killed in fighting during the month-long US military siege of the Sunni Muslim city of Fallujah. In one horrific event at the end of March, four Blackwater private security employees were killed in Fallujah. The mutilated bodies of at least two of the men were hung from a bridge over the Euphrates River.[13]

Through the summer and into the fall, fighting continued against the extremists led by al-Sadr. By the second week of September, American military deaths topped one thousand. Pentagon officials said that insurgents controlled important parts of central Iraq, including Ramadi, Fallujah, Baquba, and Samarra. These cities were in the so-called Sunni triangle, west and north of Baghdad, where Saddam Hussein remained popular. Many forces loyal to Saddam had gained strength, and it was unclear when American and Iraqi forces would be able to secure those areas. In early November, more than ten thousand American troops joined newly trained Iraqi forces for a decisive push to regain Fallujah.

The US military reported that twelve hundred insurgents had been killed and one thousand captured; Americans suffered seventy-one deaths. Residents began

In 2004, Shiite Muslims in Iraq protested against US involvement. It was just one of the signs of growing unrest in the region after the removal of Saddam.

returning to the city in the middle of December; however, it was estimated that more than half of Fallujah's thirty-nine thousand homes were damaged, and about ten thousand of those were destroyed. Even as late as the end of 2016, Fallujah was experiencing unrest. Although the city was not controlled by extremists at this time, booby-trapped vehicles exploded in the city in December 2016, leading Iraqi security forces to impose a curfew.

Still, as instability increased, Bush achieved a major step toward a democratic government in Iraq when elections were held in January 2005. An estimated eight million people came out to vote for a Transitional National Assembly despite death threats, mortar rounds, and suicide

Iraqis proudly showed their purple ink-stained fingers—a sign of pride that they had voted in the first free general election in fifty years.

bombers. Voters marked their index fingers with purple ink as a way of showing they had voted—these purple ink-stained fingers became a symbol of pride for a people who were celebrating their first free elections in Iraq in fifty years.[14]

The parliament selected Kurdish leader Jalal Talabani as president and Ibrahim al-Jaafari, a Shia, as prime minister. The Kurds were also able to establish control over their traditional homeland in northern Iraq. Masoud Barzani became the regional president of Iraqi Kurdistan.

Almost parallel with this progress came instability. South of Baghdad in February 2005, a car bomb killed 114, and more such explosions and shootings followed with 364 civilian deaths in April and 672 in May. By October 2005, the number of servicemen killed in Iraq reached 2,000. Also that month, the trials for Saddam Hussein for crimes against humanity while he led the country started. A year later, he was sentenced to death by hanging for the killing of 148 Shiites. When he received the verdict, he shouted, "Long live the people! Long live the Arab nation! Down with the spies! God is great!" He was executed by hanging on December 30, 2006.

A NEW IRAQ MOVES
FORWARD AS UNREST
CONTINUES

**"I'm a gut player. I play by instincts.
I don't play by the book."**

In mid-December, elections for the Iraqi Parliament were held, and an estimated eleven million people came out to vote, including Sunnis. Bush and his administration were pleased because they had long upheld that "the democratic process would begin to draw ordinary Sunnis away from the insurgency and encourage them to support democracy," according to the *New York Times*.[1] Iraqis even voted in violence-wracked cities like Ramadi, Fallujah, Hīt, and Husayba. Citizens brought their children to see the vote. Some dressed in their finest clothes.

While Bush was pleased with this election, he felt that he was losing power. He wrote: "Just a year earlier, I had won reelection with more votes than any candidate in

Bush made a lot of tough decisions related to the wars in Afghanistan and Iraq. These decisions opened him up to criticism from some people.

history. By the end of 2005, much of my political capital was gone."[2]

A major contributor to his loss of influence was the seemingly unending violence in Iraq. In February 2006, two large bombs destroyed the Golden Mosque in Samarra, a holy site of the Shia. Hundreds died, and Bush understood the gravity of the assault. He wrote in his memoir that the Golden Mosque was one of the holiest sites to the Shia. He compared it to an attack on St. Peter's Basilica. "This is the equivalent of your 9/11," the influential Shia leader Abdul Aziz al-Hakim told Bush.[3] The United Nations found that the death rate of civilians reached about one hundred per day in May and June. General George Casey was leading the troops in Iraq, and he was convinced that the troop presence created a sense of occupation, "which inflamed violence and fueled insurgency."[4]

In April 2006, Jawad al-Maliki was elected as the new prime minister. Sunni Arab leaders even supported him, although he had been a backer of strict policies intended to keep former supporters of Saddam's Sunni-dominated government out of power, according to the *New York Times*.[5] He had pushed for de-Ba'athification, a program to remove former Ba'ath Party members from important jobs in post-invasion Iraq. Critics assert that his actions to limit Kurdish and Sunni power ultimately led to more instability in the region.

By the summer of 2006, Bush received another blow when the Supreme Court held that some parts of the war on terror had been illegal and all the prisoners at Guantanamo were entitled to protections under the Geneva Conventions. One piece of good news came when an airstrike killed the

Jawad al-Maliki served as the prime minister of Iraq from 2006 to 2014. Critics said he did little to create an inclusive government, which led to more turmoil.

al-Qaeda leader in Iraq, Abu Musab al-Zarqawi, although Osama bin Laden still remained elusive.

America Tires of War

The death toll climbed in September as three thousand civilians were killed in that single month. In the worst attack on Baghdad since the invasion began, car bombings slaughtered two hundred people in November. (By the end of 2006, the United Nations found that thirty-four thousand civilians had died from violence that year.) Rice told Bush: "Mr. President, what we are doing is not working—really not working. It is failing."[6] The war seemed to sway the American public as midterm elections came in November 2006.

That year, Democrats took control of the House of Representatives and the Senate. Bush said after Election Day, "It was a thumping." By the end of the year, American military deaths reached three thousand and Bush's popularity fell to 22 percent, according to a CBS News/ *New York Times* poll. The poll rated him as one of the most unpopular departing presidents in history.[7]

According to the book *Presidents and Their Times: George W. Bush*, an intelligence report went against Bush's claims that the war in Iraq was making the world safer from terrorism. It said that a growing number of Muslims were now eager to fight jihad against the United States.[8]

After the midterm election, Bush felt he had to shake things up. Rumsfeld resigned as secretary of defense and was replaced by former CIA chief Robert Gates. And despite a growing discontentment with the war in Iraq, Bush decided on a new Iraq strategy by sending twenty thousand more US troops to beef up security at the beginning of 2007. Still, each month brought new car and suicide bombings, which often killed hundreds. The additional troops helped in time, but the costs in life grew before they went down. In March 2008, the death toll of service members reached four thousand, many of them killed by improvised explosive devices.

In September, however, the heartland of the Sunni insurgency, Anbar, was back under control, and American soldiers handed the region over to the Iraqi army and police force. It was a true turning point and a sign that progress was being made. Civilian deaths dropped from more than 1,600 a month in 2006 to 321 per month in mid-2008, according to James Mann's biography on Bush.

While the surge had been effective, problems were growing on the home front for Bush during his last year in office. The worst economic recession since World War II started in December 2007. Firms lost huge amounts of money because of bad mortgage loans on homes. Economists called it the bursting of the $8 trillion housing bubble. The housing crisis spread swiftly as families could not meet mortgage payments and the value of homes fell. Several large banks failed. In the fall of 2008, Congress approved a bill for $700 billion to save struggling financial companies. Consumer spending and business investment dried up, which in turn led to enormous job losses. From February 2008 to February 2010, 8.7 million Americans lost their jobs. The recession and war helped pave the way for Barack Obama to win the presidency, although he had to deal with major problems of the economy and the unrest in Afghanistan and Iraq when he took office.

During his last year in office, Bush also negotiated agreements with the Iraqi prime minister, Jawad al-Maliki, outlining plans for the United States to stay in Iraq; the plan was to pull out most troops by the summer of 2009 but also to set a deadline for all US troops to leave by the end of 2011. When American troops started to withdraw on June 30, 2009, the prime minister praised the move as a further step toward sovereignty, and cities had parades and fireworks to celebrate.

"Today's vote affirms the growth of Iraq's democracy and increasing ability to secure itself," Bush said in a statement. "Two years ago this day seemed unlikely but the

The Shoe-Hurling Incident

On his farewell visit to Iraq on December 14, 2008, George W. Bush was speaking at a press conference in Baghdad when an Iraqi journalist stood up and threw both his shoes at him—one after the other. He yelled in Arabic, "This is a farewell ... you dog!" Bush successfully ducked being hit. Shoe throwing is a highly offensive insult in the Middle East. Bush quipped, "That was a size 10 shoe he threw at me, you may want to know." While some approved of the journalist's shoe-hurling outburst as a protest against American intervention, others condemned the action because the United States and Iraq had been actively working toward peace. Still, the episode came to represent the continued differences that existed in the country.[9]

success of the surge and the courage of the Iraqi people set the conditions for these two agreements to be negotiated and approved by the Iraqi Parliament."[10]

Bush's Legacy

The legacy of President Bush's launching of a preemptive war in Iraq is still to be determined. Not finding any weapons of mass destruction certainly undercut the mission. The United States officially occupied Iraq for eight years—longer than the country's involvement in World War II. The occupation cost 4,491 American lives and cost an estimated $2 trillion—twenty times the original estimated cost.

On August 31, 2010, President Barack Obama declared an end to the seven-year combat mission in Iraq, but instability was still to come, and thousands of troops were kept on for security training. On December 15, 2011, the United States declared a formal end to operations in Iraq, but peace was not that simple to maintain. In the fall of 2016, Obama sent additional troops into Iraq, bringing the count of US soldiers there up to about five thousand, but that was far less than the peak of one hundred and seventy thousand in 2007. At that time, an estimated thirty thousand Iraqi and US-led coalition forces had been battling to take cities back from ISIS (the Islamic State of Iraq and Syria), who started to take over part of Iraq in 2014. Mosul is home to about two million residents, and it is the last major stronghold of the terrorist organization. Mosul had been a thriving industrial city and an important hub for goods that flowed between Turkey and Syria. ISIS was able to take control of the city in just a few days in June 2014. As of this writing, ISIS had lost posts in Fallujah and Ramadi. The British newspaper the *Sun* said that some analysts believe regaining Mosul would spell the end for ISIS in Iraq altogether, and the group would effectively be confined to Syria.[11]

While these have been positive steps toward keeping Iraq secure, many view the region as unstable. Bush has stood by his decision to remove Saddam Hussein, believing that the world would be worse off with Saddam in power. He does leave a legacy of calming, assuring, and uniting a country after one of the most deadly attacks on American soil. Also, his charge to fight in Afghanistan was in direct response to an attack on the United States.

Some critics have said that Bush's war in Iraq may have strengthened Iran as well. As the United States followed through on the Bush plans to remove troops from Iraq, Iran offered support. Iran reportedly sold Iraq over $10 billion in weapons. A 2015 article in the *Atlantic* quoted Iraqi lawmaker Mohammed al-Karbouly saying that "Iran now dominates Iraq."[12] Iran has been seen as a threat in the region, but prime minister of Britain Theresa May stressed the importance of the deal struck in 2015 to neutralize the possibility of the country acquiring nuclear weapons and to counteract any of Iran's "aggressive regional actions," according to the BBC. [13]

And in Afghanistan, the reports showed that the fighting between the Taliban and government forces had escalated. The Taliban had pushed back and seized a number of district centers and threatened other provincial capitals. In 2015, the United Nations deemed nearly half of the country's provinces as being at high or extreme risk.[14]

In some regards, Bush will always be seen as a strong leader who led the country with strength and grace after the biggest terrorist attack ever on American soil. He understood the value of compassion and unity, reaching out to Muslim American citizens when prejudices ran high. How history will judge the wars that followed is yet to be determined. As the Miller Center, a nonpartisan institute that seeks to expand understanding of the presidency, policy, and political history for the nation's governance challenges, summed it up: "The legacy of George W. Bush remains, much like his 2000 election, a subject of profound controversy, and any truly objective evaluation will likely be years in the future … His administration was overshadowed by the wars in Afghanistan and Iraq. President Bush's place in US history will be debated and reconsidered for many years to come."[15]

CHRONOLOGY

July 6, 1946

George Bush is born in New Haven, Connecticut.

February 24, 1991

First Gulf War begins.

November 2000

Bush wins disputed presidential election against Al Gore.

September 11, 2001

Attacks on World Trade Center and Pentagon.

September 18, 2001

Bush signs resolution authorizing use of force against those who attacked United States.

September 20, 2001

Bush speaks before joint session of Congress; declares war on terror.

October 7, 2001

US-led attack on Afghanistan begins.

November 14, 2001

Alliance forces take over capital of Kabul and control almost all of the north of Afghanistan.

December 5, 2001

Interim government established with Hamid Karzai as interim head; creates international peacekeeping force.

December 9, 2001

The Taliban collapses after surrender of Kandahar.

December 12–17, 2001

Battle of Tora Bora against Taliban and al-Qaeda fighters; Osama bin Laden escapes.

March 2002

Operation Anaconda, a major battle against al-Qaeda ensues.

June 1, 2002

In graduation speech at West Point, Bush says to be ready for preemptive action when necessary.

June 2002

Transition Afghanistan government is named.

November 8, 2002

UN Security Council under Resolution 1441 approves a resolution on Iraq, forcing Saddam Hussein to disarm or face "serious consequences."

March 17, 2003

Bush addresses nation warning of plans to invade, giving Saddam Hussein forty-eight hours to leave Iraq.

March 20, 2003

Bush announces start of war against Iraq.

April 9, 2003

Saddam Hussein's rule collapses as US troops take control of Baghdad.

May 1, 2003

The United States declares that major combat is over; Bush delivers speech on USS *Abraham Lincoln* in front of "Mission Accomplished" banner.

July 2, 2003

Bush challenges terrorists, saying "Bring 'em on!" as violence escalates in Iraq.

December 13, 2003

Saddam Hussein is captured.

January 2004

Afghanistan approves its first constitution.

June 28, 2004

Iraq gets formal sovereignty.

September 7, 2004

American military deaths surpasses one thousand.

October 6, 2004

Official Iraq Survey Group report concludes that Saddam Hussein did not possess weapons of mass destruction.

October 9, 2004

Hamid Karzai becomes the first democratically elected head of Afghanistan.

January 30, 2005

Iraq has first free elections in fifty years.

March 31, 2005

The Commission on the Intelligence Capabilities of the United States Regarding Weapons of Mass Destruction reports that intelligence was "dead wrong" about Iraq's weapons of mass destruction capabilities before the US invasion.

February 22, 2006

A powerful bomb destroys the Askariya Shrine in Samarra, one of Iraq's most revered Shiite shrines—another episode of ongoing violence.

December 30, 2006

Saddam Hussein is hanged.

March 23, 2008

The American death toll for soldiers reaches four thousand.

January 20, 2009

George W. Bush's last day in office.

June 30, 2009

American troops start to withdraw from Iraq.

December 15, 2011

US forces declare formal end to operations in Iraq.

May 2, 2011

Osama bin Laden killed by US forces in Pakistan.

September 28, 2016

President Obama sends six hundred more troops to help Iraq retake Mosul from ISIS. Additional troops bring number of soldiers in Iraq to five thousand.

CHAPTER NOTES

INTRODUCTION

1. George W. Bush's First Inaugural Address, bartleby.com, http://www.bartleby.com/124/pres66.html.
2. The White House, Office of the Press Secretary, "Statement by the President on the End of the Combat Mission in Afghanistan," December 28, 2014, https://www.whitehouse. gov/the-press-office/2014/12/28/statement-president-end-combat-mission-afghanistan.
3. Jane Onyamga-Omara, "U.S. Service Members, Civilians Killed in Afghanistan," *USA Today*, November 3, 2016, http:// www.usatoday.com/story/news/world/2016/11/03/two-us-service-members-killed-afghanistan/93227064/.
4. "George W. Bush: Traits and Instincts," *Frontline*, PBS.org, http://www.pbs.org/wgbh/pages/frontline/shows/choice 2004/bush/traits.html.

CHAPTER 1 THE AGE OF TERRORISM BEGINS

1. Tim Padgett, "The Interrupted Reading: The Kids with George W. Bush on 9/11," *Time*, May 3, 2011, http://content .time.com/time/magazine/article/0,9171,2069582,00.html.
2. "We're the Only Plane in the Sky," *Politico*, September 9, 2016, http://www.politico.com/magazine/story/2016/09/were-the-only-plane-in-the-sky-214230.
3. Ely Brown, "Florida Students Witnessed the Moment Bush Learned of 9/11 Terror Attacks," ABC News, September 8, 2011, http://abcnews.go.com/US/September_11/florida-students-witnessed-moment-bush-learned-911-terror/ story?id=14474518.
4. "Text of Bush's Address to the Nation After Terrorist Attacks on New York and Washington, CNN.com, September 11, 2001, http://edition.cnn.com/2001/US/09/11/bush. speech.text/.

5. "FAQ About 9/11," 9/11 Memorial & Museum, https://www.911memorial.org/faq-about-911.
6. "Afghanistan Profile—Timeline," BBC, November 21, 2016, http://www.bbc.com/news/world-south-asia-12024253.
7. Alexandra Poolos, "Afghanistan: The Taliban's Rise to Power," Radio Free Europe, September 18, 2001, http://www.rferl.org/a/1097442.html.
8. "Taliban," Encyclopedia.com, http://www.encyclopedia.com/history/asia-and-africa/central-asian-history/taliban.
9. "This Day in History: U.S.-Led Attack on Afghanistan Begins," History Channel, http://www.history.com/this-day-in-history/u-s-led-attack-on-afghanistan-begins.
10. "Al-Qaida Timeline: Plots and Attacks," NBC News, http://www.nbcnews.com/id/4677978/ns/world_news-hunt_for_al_qaida/t/al-qaida-timeline-plots-attacks/#.WDO2APPFmL0.
11. Gary Hart, "Unheeded Warnings: George W. Bush and 9/11," *National Interest*, October 17, 2005, http://nationalinterest.org/feature/unheeded-warnings-george-w-bush-9-11-14122.
12. Julian Borger, "Bush Team 'Agreed Plan to Attack the Taliban the Day Before September 11,'" *Guardian*, March 24, 2004, https://www.theguardian.com/world/2004/mar/24/september11.usa2.
13. "Gulf War Ground Offensive Begins," This Day in History, History Channel, http://www.history.com/this-day-in-history/gulf-war-ground-offensive-begins.
14. "Persian Gulf War," History Channel, http://www.history.com/topics/persian-gulf-war.
15. Michael Carlson, "General Norman Schwarzkopf Obituary," *Guardian*, December 28, 2012, https://www.theguardian.com/world/2012/dec/28/norman-schwarzkopf.
16. "The Persian Gulf War," American Experience, http://www.pbs.org/wgbh/americanexperience/features/general-article/bush-gulf-war/.

17. "The Election of 1992," American Experience, http://www.pbs.org/wgbh/americanexperience/features/general-article/bush-election92/.
18. William J. Clinton, "Statement on Signing the Iraq Liberation Act of 1998," October 31, 1998, http://www.presidency.ucsb.edu/ws/?pid=55205.
19. George W. Bush First Inaugural address, January 20, 2001, http://www.thisnation.com/library/inaugural/gwbush.html.
20. Ibid.
21. "Tenet Played Major Role in War on Terrorism," *Washington Post*, June 3, 2004, http://www.washingtonpost.com/wp-srv/nation/tenet_background.html.

CHAPTER 2 SETTING THE STAGE FOR WAR

1. "September 11th Hijackers Fast Facts," CNN, http://www.cnn.com/2013/07/27/us/september-11th-hijackers-fast-facts/.
2. "'Islam Is Peace,' says President," White House, September 17, 2001, https://georgewbush-whitehouse.archives.gov/news/releases/2001/09/20010917-11.html.
3. George W. Bush Presidential Library and Museum, http://www.georgewbushlibrary.smu.edu/en/Visit/Exhibits/Featured-Artifact.aspx.
4. "Presidential Approval Ratings—George W. Bush," Gallup, http://www.gallup.com/poll/116500/presidential-approval-ratings-george-bush.aspx.
5. "Statement by the North Atlantic Council," September 12, 2001, NATO, http://www.nato.int/docu/pr/2001/p01-124e.htm.
6. George W. Bush, *Decision Points* (New York: Random House, 2010), p. 191.

7. Sally Donnelly, "The Day the FAA Stopped the World," *Time*, September 14, 2001, http://content.time.com/time/nation/article/0,8599,174912,00.html.

8. Matt Meltzer, "A Brief (and Totally Fascinating) History of Airport Security," Thrillist, July 14, 2015, https://www.thrillist.com/travel/nation/why-do-we-have-to-take-our-shoes-off-at-airport-security-history-of-the-tsa.

9. "Transcript of President Bush's Address," CNN, September 21, 2001, http://edition.cnn.com/2001/US/09/20/gen.bush.transcript/.

10. "Ridge Says He Was Pressured to Raise Terror Alert," NBC News, August 20, 2009, http://www.nbcnews.com/id/32501273/ns/us_news-security/t/ridge-says-he-was-pressured-raise-terror-alert/#.WFGJkPPFmL0.

11. "Timeline: How the Anthrax Scare Unfolded," NPR, February 15, 2011, http://www.npr.org/2011/02/15/93170200/timeline-how-the-anthrax-terror-unfolded.

12. Ed Grabianowski, "How the Patriot Act Works," HowStuffWorks.com, http://people.howstuffworks.com/patriot-act.htm.

13. Robert S. Mueller testimony, Federal Bureau of Investigation, May 24, 2004, https://archives.fbi.gov/archives/news/testimony/usa-patriot-act.

CHAPTER 3 THE BATTLE AGAINST THE TALIBAN

1. George W. Bush, *Decision Points* (New York: Random House, 2010), p. 194.

2. Ibid.

3. Bush, 196.

4. "Bush Rejects Taliban Offer to Hand Bin Laden Over," *Guardian*, October 14, 2001, https://www.theguardian.com/world/2001/oct/14/afghanistan.terrorism5.

5. Bush, p. 199.

6. James Meeks, "Freedom, Job—and Fear," *Guardian*, November 13, 2001, https://www.theguardian.com/world/2001/nov/14/afghanistan.terrorism.

7. Timothy Bella and Benjamin Fearnow, "Remembering America's Second Deadliest Place Crash," *Atlantic*, November 11, 2011, http://www.theatlantic.com/national/archive/2011/11/remembering-americas-second-deadliest-plane-crash/248313/.

8. Biography of Hamid Karzai, Office of the President, Islamic Republic of Afghanistan, http://president.gov.af/en/page/1043.

9. "Omar, Taliban Flee Kandahar," CNN, December 7, 2001, http://www.cnn.com/2001/US/12/07/ret.frontlines.facts/index.html.

10. Mary Anne Weaver, "Lost at Tora Bora," *New York Times Magazine*, September 11, 2005.

11. Ibid.

12. "War in Afghanistan: Battle of Tora Bora," About.com, August 4, 2015, http://militaryhistory.about.com/od/afghanistan/p/torabora.htm.

13. "March 2002: Operation Anaconda," *Frontline*, PBS, http://www.pbs.org/wgbh/pages/frontline/shows/campaign/etc/epilogue.html.

14. "Operation Anaconda," GlobalSecurity.org, http://www.globalsecurity.org/military/ops/oef-anaconda.htm.

CHAPTER 4 REBUILDING AFGHANISTAN

1. George W. Bush, *Decision Points* (New York: Random House, 2010), p. 208.

2. Gary Tuchman, "Karzai Elected as Afghan Leader," CNN, June 13, 2002, http://www.cnn.com/2002/WORLD/asiapcf/central/06/13/afghan.council/.

3. "Afghan Civilians," Watson Institute of International and Public Affairs at Brown University, Updated August 2016, http://watson.brown.edu/costsofwar/costs/human/civilians/afghan.

4. "Assassination Attempt in Afghanistan Latest of Several," CNN, September 5, 2002, http://edition.cnn.com/2002/WORLD/asiapcf/central/09/05/afghan.recent.attacks/.

5. "NATO Increases Number of Troops in Afghanistan," BBC, http://www.bbc.co.uk/history/events/nato_increases_the_number_of_troops_in_afghanistan.

6. "Hamid Karzai," Encyclopaedia Britannica, updated December 7, 2016, https://www.britannica.com/biography/Hamid-Karzai.

7. Bush, p. 209.

8. Mujib Mashal and Eric Schmitt, "Afghan Security Crisis Sets Stage for Terrorists' Resurgence," *New York Times*, December 2, 2016, http://www.nytimes.com/2016/12/02/world/asia/afghanistan-security-terrorism-taliban.html.

9. Bush, p. 215.

10. "Khalid Sheik Mohammed Fast Facts," CNN Library, December 9, 2015, http://www.cnn.com/2013/02/03/world/meast/khalid-sheikh-mohammed-fast-facts/.Ibid., 215.

11. Bush, p. 215.

12. Mark Landler, "Obama Says He Will Keep More Troops in Afghanistan Than Planned," *New York Times,* July 6, 2016, http://www.nytimes.com/2016/07/07/world/asia/obama-afghanistan-troops.html

CHAPTER 5 A PIVOT TO IRAQ

1. "US and British Support for Hussein Regime," Global Policy Forum, https://www.globalpolicy.org/iraq-conflict-the-historical-background-/us-and-british-support-for-huss-regime.html.

2. Michael Lipka, "The Sunni-Shia Divide: Where They Live, What They Believe and How They View Each Other," Pew Research Center, June 18, 2014, http://www.pewresearch.org/fact-tank/2014/06/18/the-sunni-shia-divide-where-they-live-what-they-believe-and-how-they-view-each-other/.

3. T. Morad, *Iraq's Last Jews: Stories of Daily Life, Upheaval, and Escape from Modern Babylon* (Basingstoke, UK: Palgrave Macmillan), 2008.

4. Patrick Martin, "Explainer: Shia-Sunni Divide and Iraq's Deadly Sectarian War," *Globe and Mail*, June 25, 2014, http://www.theglobeandmail.com/news/world/sunni---shia-divide-explained/article19337058/.

5. Tewfik Cassis, "A Brief History of ISIS," *The Week*, November 21, 2015, http://theweek.com/articles/589924/brief-history-isis.

6. Helene Cooper, "U.S. to Send 600 More Troops to Iraq to Retake Mosul from ISIS," *New York Times*, September 28, 2016, http://www.nytimes.com/2016/09/29/world/middleeast/obama-troops-iraq.html.

7. "President Clinton Explains Iraq strike," CNN, December 16, 1998, http://www.cnn.com/ALLPOLITICS/stories/1998/12/16/transcripts/clinton.html.

8. "Iraq War," Encyclopaedia Britannica, https://www.britannica.com/event/Iraq-War.

9. George W. Bush, *Decision Points* (New York: Random House, 2010), p. 235.

10. Julian Borger, "There Were No Weapons of Mass Destruction," *Guardian*, October 7, 2004, https://www.theguardian.com/world/2004/oct/07/usa.iraq1.

11. James Mann, *George W. Bush* (New York: Henry Holt and Company, 2015).

12. Brent Scowcroft, "Don't Attack Saddam," *Wall Street Journal*, August 15, 2002, http://www.wsj.com/articles/SB1029371773228069195.

13. Bush, p. 239.

CHAPTER 6 A SHORT WAR BUT A LINGERING BATTLE

1. "November 8, 2002," On This Day, http://www.onthisday.com/date/2002/november/8.
2. "Iraq and Weapons of Mass Destruction," National Security Archive, updated February 11, 2004, http://nsarchive.gwu.edu/NSAEBB/NSAEBB80/.
3. Jim Miklaszewski, "Avoiding Attacking Suspected Terrorist Mastermind," *NBC Nightly News*, March 2, 2004, http://www.nbcnews.com/id/4431601/ns/nbc_nightly_news_with_brian_williams/t/avoiding-attacking-suspected-terrorist-mastermind/#.WFLNivPFmL0.
4. George W. Bush, *Decision Points* (New York: Random House, 2010), p. 243.
5. Edith Lederer, "Blix Says No Smoking Guns Found in Iraq," Global Policy Forum, January 9, 2003, https://www.globalpolicy.org/component/content/article/168/37569.html.
6. Colin Powell, "Briefing on the Iraq Weapons Inspectors' 60-Day Report: Iraqi Non-cooperation and Defiance of the UN," US Department of State, January 27, 2003, http://nsarchive.gwu.edu/NSAEBB/NSAEBB80/new/doc%2021/Briefing%20on%20the%20Iraq%20Weapons%20Inspectors'%20Report.htm.
7. "Text of President Bush's 2003 State of the Union Address," *Washington Post*, January 28, 2003, http://www.washingtonpost.com/wp-srv/onpolitics/transcripts/bushtext_012803.html.
8. Bush, p. 242.
9. "Full Text of Colin Powell's Speech," *Guardian*, February 5, 2003, https://www.theguardian.com/world/2003/feb/05/iraq.usa.

10. Bush, George W., *Decision Points* (New York: Random House, 2010), p. 247.

11. Ishaan Tharoor, "Viewpoint: Why Was the Biggest Protest in World History Ignored?" *Time*, February 15, 2013, http://world.time.com/2013/02/15/viewpoint-why-was-the-biggest-protest-in-world-history-ignored/.

12. "Bush on Iraq," *Washington Post*, March 17, 2003, http://www.washingtonpost.com/wp-srv/onpolitics/transcripts/bushtext_031703.html.

13. David E. Sanger with John F. Burns, "Bush Declares Start of Iraq War; Missile Said to Be Aimed at Hussein," *New York Times*, March 20, 2003, http://www.nytimes.com/2003/03/20/international/worldspecial/bush-declares-start-of-iraq-war-missile-said-to.html.

14. William Schneider, "The Head of the Snake," *Atlantic*, April 1, 2003, http://www.theatlantic.com/politics/archive/2003/04/the-head-of-the-snake/377855/.

15. "Bush Declares War," CNN, March 19, 2003, http://www.cnn.com/2003/US/03/19/sprj.irq.int.bush.transcript/.

16. Matthew Cox, "Army Sgt. 1st Class Paul R. Smith," *Military Times*, April 4, 2003, http://thefallen.militarytimes.com/army-sgt-1st-class-paul-r-smith/256561.

CHAPTER 7 MISSION ACCOMPLISHED?: THE POST-WAR BLUES

1. "Bush Makes Historic Speech Sboard Warship," CNN, May 1, 2003, http://www.cnn.com/2003/US/05/01/bush transcript/.

2. Robert Poole, "Looting Iraq," *Smithsonian Magazine*, February 2008.

3. Paul Bremer, "I Ran Iraq in 2003. Washington Hadn't Prepared for the Aftermath of War," *Guardian*, July 6, 2016,

https://www.theguardian.com/commentisfree/2016/jul/06/iraq-war-aftermath-paul-bremer.

4. Mark Thompson, "How Disbanding the Iraqi Army Fueled ISIS," *Time*, May 28, 2015, http://time.com/3900753/isis-iraq-syria-army-united-states-mil.

5. Dina al-Shibeeb, "Where Is Iraq's Baath Party Today?" Al Arabiya News, August 21, 2015, http://english.alarabiya.net/en/perspective/analysis/2015/08/21/Where-is-Iraq-s-Baath-party-today-.html.

6. Jonathan Steele, "Ahmed Chalabi obituary," *Guardian*, November 4, 2015, https://www.theguardian.com/world/2015/nov/04/ahmed-chalabi.

7. Dexter Filkins and Richard A. Oppel Jr., "After the War: Truck Bombing; Huge Suicide Blast Demolishes U.N. Headquarters in Baghdad; Top Aid Officials Among 17 Dead," *New York Times*, August 20, 2003, http://www.nytimes.com/2003/08/20/world/after-war-truck-bombing-huge-suicide-blast-demolishes-un-headquarters-baghdad.html.

8. "Najaf Bombing Kills Shiite Leader, Followers Say," CNN, August 30, 2003, http://www.cnn.com/2003/WORLD/meast/08/29/sprj.irq.najaf/index.html?iref=mpstoryview.

9. George W. Bush, *Decision Points* (New York: Random House, 2010), p. 262.

10. Bush, p. 268.

11. "Iraq Prison Abuse Scandal," CNN Library, updated March 12, 2016, http://www.cnn.com/2013/10/30/world/meast/iraq-prison-abuse-scandal-fast-facts/.

12. Dexter Filkins, "Extent of Government's Control Unclear as It Formally Steps In," *New York Times*, June 28, 2004, http://www.nytimes.com/2004/06/28/international/extent-of-governments-control-unclear-as-it-formally-steps-in.html?_r=0.

13. Jeffrey Gettleman, "Enraged Mob in Fallujah Kills 4 American Contractors," *New York Times*, March 31, 2004, http://www.

nytimes.com/2004/03/31/international/worldspecial/
enraged-mob-in-falluja-kills-4-american.html.

14. Christopher Woolf, "The Purple Finger Remains a Hopeful
Symbol in Iraq, as Iraqis Go to the Polls," PRI.org, April 30,
2014, http://www.pri.org/stories/2014-04-30/purple-finger-
remains-hopeful-symbol-iraq-iraqis-go-polls.

CHAPTER 8 A NEW IRAQ MOVES FORWARD AS UNREST CONTINUES

1. Dexter Filkins, "Iraqis, including Sunnis, Vote in Large
Numbers," *New York Times*, December 16, 2005, http://
www.nytimes.com/2005/12/16/world/middleeast/iraqis-
including-sunnis-vote-in-large-numbers.html.
2. George W. Bush, *Decision Points* (New York: Random House,
2010), p. 330.
3. Bush, p. 361.
4. Bush, p. 362.
5. Richard A. Oppel, "Shiites Settle on Pick for Iraqi Premier,"
New York Times, April 22, 2006, http://www.nytimes.
com/2006/04/22/world/middleeast/shiites-settle-on-pick-
for-iraqi-premier.html.
6. Condoleezza Rice, *No Higher Honor: A Memoir of My Years in
Washington* (New York: Broadway Paperbacks, 2012), p. 515.
7. "Bush's Final Approval Rating: 22 Percent," CBS News,
January 16, 2009, http://www.cbsnews.com/news/bushs-
final-approval-rating-22-percent/.
8. Michael Burgan, *Presidents and Their Times: George W. Bush*
(Tarrytown, NY: Marshall Cavendish, 2012), p. 75.
9. "Iraqi Journalist Throws Shoes at Bush in Baghdad," CNN,
December 15, 2008, http://www.cnn.com/2008/WORLD/
meast/12/14/bush.iraq/.

10. "Bush Praises Approval of Iraq-US Security Pact," *Washington Post*, November 27, 2008, http://www.washingtonpost.com/wp-dyn/content/article/2007/08/27/AR2007082700834.html.

11. Felix Allen and Jennifer Hale, "Attack on ISIS: Battle for Mosul Begins – Where IS the Iraqi City, How Did ISIS Take Control and How Long Will the Assault Last?" *Sun*, October 17, 2016, https://www.thesun.co.uk/news/1975545/battle-mosul-isis-assault/.

12. Conor Friedersdorf, "How Foreign Policy Hawks Emboldened Iran," *Atlantic*, January 14, 2015, http://www.theatlantic.com/international/archive/2015/01/how-foreign-policy-hawks-empowered-iran/384500/.

13. "Theresa May 'Clear-Eyed' Over Iran Threat," BBC, December 7, 2016, http://www.bbc.com/news/uk-politics-38227680.

14. "Afghanistan: Events of 2015," Human Rights Watch, https://www.hrw.org/world-report/2016/country-chapters/afghanistan.

15. "George W. Bush: Impact and Legacy," The Miller Center, http://millercenter.org/president/biography/gwbush-impact-and-legacy.

GLOSSARY

adherent Someone who supports a certain person, party, or set of ideas.

anthrax A serious potentially deadly infection caused by the bacterium *Bacillus anthracis*.

caliphate An Islamic state that is led by a caliph, a political and religious leader whose power and authority is absolute.

coalition An alliance of political groups or countries formed to oppose a common foe or pursue a common goal.

cruise missile A low-flying missile that is guided to its target by an onboard computer.

disarmament The reduction or withdrawal of military forces and weapons.

extremist A person who holds extreme or fanatical political or religious views, especially one who resorts to or advocates extreme action, such as violence.

HAZMAT Hazardous material that would be a danger to life or to the environment if released without precautions.

IED (improvised explosive device) A simple bomb made and used by unofficial or unauthorized forces.

infrared Producing or using rays of light that cannot be seen and that are longer than rays that produce red light.

insurgent A rebel or person who rises in forcible opposition to lawful authority.

intelligence In terms of government, information that supports law enforcement, national security, military, and foreign policy objectives.

jihad In the Islamic religion, a war or struggle against unbelievers.

Shia The second-largest branch of Islam after Sunni Islam. Adherents follow the teachings of the prophet Muhammad and the religious guidance of his family.

sovereign Descirbes a nation that is independent and has supreme authority or power over itself.

Sunni The largest branch of Islam; Sunnis make up about 80 percent of the Muslim population in the world. The Sunni maintain that the Muslim community must select the Prophet's successor (caliph) to lead.

FURTHER READING

BOOKS

Burgan, Michael. *Presidents and Their Times: George W. Bush*. Tarrytown, NY: Marshall Cavendish, 2012.

Bush, George W. *Decision Points*. New York, NY: Random House, 2010.

Mann, James. *George W. Bush*. New York, NY: Henry Holt and Company, 2015.

Marquez, Herón. *George W. Bush*. Minneapolis, MN: Lerner Publications, 2006

WEBSITES

Embassy of the Republic of Iraq
http://www.iraqiembassy.us
> *This website offers information on current government affairs in Iraq.*

George W. Bush Presidential Library and Museum
https://www.georgewbushlibrary.smu.edu
> *The library and museum serve as a resource for the study of the life and career of George W. Bush, while also promoting a better understanding of the presidency, American history, and important issues of public policy.*

9/11 Memorial & Museum
https://www.911memorial.org/museum
> *This organization reviews the implications of the events of 9/11 and documents the impact of those events, as well as explores 9/11's continuing significance.*

Office of the President, Islamic Republic of Afghanistan
http://president.gov.af/en
> This website provides information on the status of Afghanistan today.

MOVIES

The Green Zone (2010)
> Team of inspectors are on a mission to find Iraq's reported stockpile of weapons of mass destruction in 2003.

The Hurt Locker (2008)
> The story of an Iraq War Explosive Ordnance Disposal team.

Restrepo (2010)
> A documentary about one year with a platoon in the deadliest valley in Afghanistan.

INDEX